THE *Fine* PRINT

Also by Cedric Hopkins

BOOKS

Understanding Rule 32: Post-Conviction Relief Manual, Forms and Case Law

Federal Habeas Corpus Handbook: Taking Your Case from State Court to Federal Court

Black Book of Rights: A Continuation of the Civil Rights Movement

YOUTUBE

In this corner of the internet, Cedric trades ink for pixels, explaining and expanding on the NIL and Rev-Share concepts and ideas you'll find in *The Fine Print*.

WEBSITES

Want the legal side of sports, NIL, and revenue sharing? Check out:
hlosportslaw.com

And if you argue with the TV during college football & NFL games, you'll fit right in at:
fieldandcourt.net

CEDRIC HOPKINS
ATTORNEY AT LAW

THE *Fine* PRINT

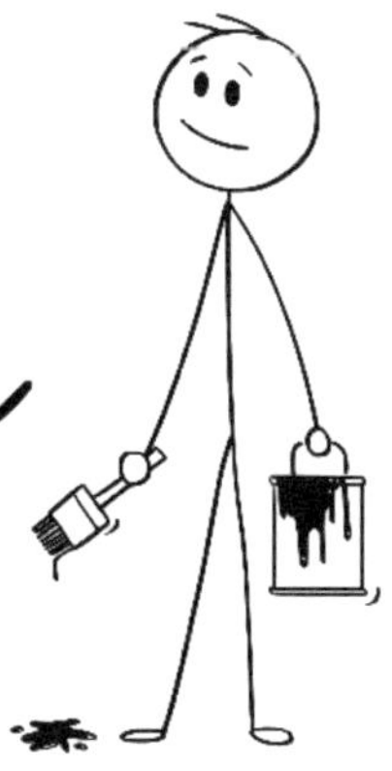

THE LAW & BUSINESS OF NIL & REVENUE SHARING FOR COLLEGE ATHLETES

HOPKINS LAW
EDUCATED & EMPOWERED ATHLETES

This book provides general information about the new legal and business landscape of college athletics, including NIL, revenue sharing, and related topics. It is offered for educational and informational purposes only and **does not constitute legal advice, financial advice, tax advice, or a guarantee of any particular legal outcome.** Readers should not act or refrain from acting on the basis of any content in this book without seeking individualized advice from a licensed attorney in the relevant jurisdiction. There is no attorney-client relationship established with Cedric Hopkins, Hopkins Law Sports Management, or The Hopkins Law Office by purchasing this book, reading it, or implementing any of the information or examples contained in it. Any communication related to this book, including questions, comments, or feedback, does not create an attorney-client relationship unless and until a separate written engagement agreement is signed by both you and Cedric Hopkins setting out the scope and terms of representation.

References in this book to real universities, conferences, teams, trademarks, logos, coaches, administrators, or athletes are for identification, commentary, and educational purposes only. The use of names, marks, and other identifiers is not intended to suggest any sponsorship, endorsement, or affiliation. The discussion of brand names and trademarks is consistent with the distinction recognized by the Supreme Court between using a mark as a source identifier and using it in an expressive or referential context. See, generally, *Jack Daniel's Properties, Inc. v. VIP Products LLC*, 599 U.S. 140 (2023).

Similarly, any discussion of real persons, their images, or performances is intended to report on and comment about matters of public concern, not to appropriate the entire commercial value of any individual's performance. See, generally, *Zacchini v. Scripps-Howard Broad. Co.*, 433 U.S. 562 (1977). The author respects intellectual property and publicity rights and does not claim any rights in third-party trademarks, copyrights, or likenesses beyond those permitted by applicable law. All non-licensed logos, marks, or other information in this book is used for fair use commentary, criticism, and educational purposes. See, generally, *Hosseinzadeh v. Klein*, 276 F.Supp.3d 34 (S.D.N.Y. 2017); *Equals Three, LLC v. Jukin Media, Inc.*, 139 F. Supp. 3d 1094 (C.D. Cal. 2015).

Nothing in this book creates an attorney–client relationship between the reader and the author, nor should any portion of this book be relied upon as a substitute for personalized legal counsel regarding specific facts, contracts, disputes, or compliance obligations.

Editors:
Cover Design: Carly, Peggy, Jamal & Amaiah
Content & Illustrations: Sam, Carly, Peggy & Isaiah

Special thanks to my wife, Carly, and my mom, Peggy, for being my biggest supporters and for seeing me through the grueling yet fun process of producing this book. To my daughter, Amaiah, for her creative insight -- sometimes savage, always honest. To my son, Isaiah, for the inspo to embark on new journeys. To my dad, Sam, for putting his mastery of the English language to work through generous edits and thoughtful feedback. And to my brother, Jamal, for always being in my corner. Thanks, y'all!

For inquires:
Hopkins Law
P.O. Box 213
Woodland, CA 95695

The intent of the author is to offer information of a general nature to help you understand the law behind NIL and Rev-Share, and to help you launch and run your business.

Library of Congress Cataloging-in-Publication Data

Paperback ISBN: 978-0-9982196-3-9
E-book ISBN: 978-0-9982196-4-6

1st Printing
1st Edition, March 2026

ABOUT THE AUTHOR

Chop arguing before the Ninth Circuit

Born and raised in Columbus, Ohio, Cedric Hopkins ("Uncle Chop") eventually found his way out to California where he passed the California Bar exam (eventually Arizona, too). Chop clerked for a judge, then opened a private practice where he advocated for children in Child Protective Services' care and for citizens charged with crimes. He has spent the better part of two decades standing between individuals and systems that are much bigger than they are, fighting to make sure their voices are heard and their constitutional rights are protected.

He has taken those fights through the state court systems (Arizona and California) and into the federal system, including arguing before the U.S. Court of Appeals for the Ninth Circuit. He's also no stranger to the U.S. Supreme Court, having worked on cases for years until SCOTUS gave him a final answer. He also occasionally steps into the classroom, teaching law students how to think critically, advocate fiercely, and stand up for those the system tends to overlook.

Before the courtroom, Chop was part of the Men's Basketball team at the University of New Mexico. You could usually find him at the end of the bench, hoping the Lobos would go up by 20 so he could sub into the game. Fun fact: For a couple of weeks in the 90's, Chop led the NCAA in points-per-minute after hitting two threes and a couple of jumpshots in garbage time. Having played DI sports, he knows all about the 6 a.m. lifts, technical film sessions, grueling travel schedules, and practice grind you face. *The Fine Print* is meant to assist with relieving the pressure of new off-the-court demands of learning NIL and Rev-Share law, launching a start-up, staying on the IRS's good side, and running a successful business. Combining his love for college sports with his passion for the law and fighting for what is right, Chop is here to serve you.

For my cousin, Dylan &
my grandma, Sonny

The Table of Contents

The Table of Contents

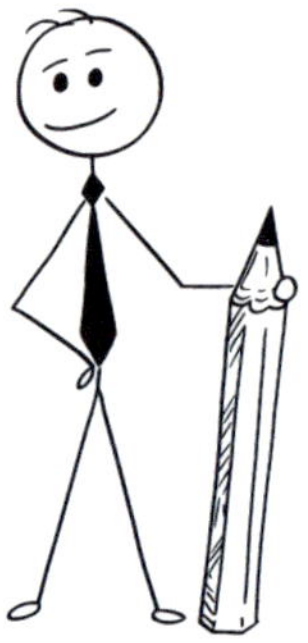

The Table of Contents

THAT'S THE END OF THE TABLE OF CONTENTS
contents conte
nts contents

MODULE ONE

THE EVOLVING MINDSET OF TODAY'S COLLEGE ATHLETES

New Era of College Sports

College sports is a business. Arguably, it's been a business from the first college sporting event. On August 3, 1852, Yale's rowing team challenged Harvard's rowing team to a race on Lake Winnipesaukee. Undoubtedly, the press covered the event. The school sold tickets and food. And there was talk among the fans and participants afterwards. Those once peripheral "game-day" activities were trivial back then, but today they account for billions of dollars. At the risk of stating the obvious, intercollegiate sports has evolved into a multi-billion dollar business. The money exchanged during the first crew race may have been inconsequential, but it was the genesis of revenue streams for universities, conferences, and what would become the NCAA.

College sports evolved from schools paying a teacher a small stipend to also coach one of their sports teams, to 28 different revenue streams feeding billions of dollars to thousands of people. It's been that way for decades. This revenue flow only became an issue when one party -- the players -- began demanding a small share of that money.

The NCAA fought for decades to prevent college athletes from getting any share of the money generated, despite their indispensable role in this revenue-generating machine. The NCAA was successful because of the "amateur" argument. Through a number of lawsuits, however, the

United States Supreme Court has recognized that the NCAA, conferences, universities, and every entity involved in college sports treats college athletics like professional sports. The argument that college sports are amateur sports is dead -- killed by the very people who are sworn to keep college athletics amateur.

So that's where we are with college sports. In 2024, the NCAA generated $1.38 billion, the Power Five Conferences generated $3.54 billion, and the individual schools brought in hundreds of millions of dollars. College athletes -- the people who actually generate that money -- were destined to start getting paid their fair share.

Educated & Empowered Athletes

This book was written with two goals in mind: 1) to educate college athletes about the business of college sports (which includes educating athletes about the laws surrounding the business); and 2) to empower college athletes to take ownership of their opportunities, protect themselves legally and financially, and confidently build a foundation for long-term success, both during and after their playing careers.

Those two goals -- education and empowerment -- will ensure you have the knowledge and know-how to protect yourself when navigating business deals with schools and companies. Once armed with the knowledge that's contained within this book, the pitfalls that could bring about legal and financial hardships are easily recognized and can be skillfully avoided. Most importantly, once you have a clear understanding of the material the Hopkins Law Sports Management team presents -- both, in this book and during in-person workshops -- you'll have the vision to turn Name, Image, and Likeness (NIL) and Revenue Sharing (Rev-Share) deals into lasting opportunities, not just quick paychecks.

Hybrid Role of Athlete & Entrepreneur

Whether you like it or not, as a college athlete today, you are not just competing on the field, court, or track -- you are stepping into a powerful new role: that of an entrepreneur. The era of solely being an athlete is over. The rise of Name, Image, and Likeness (NIL) opportunities, revenue-sharing deals, and personal branding means that, along with being an athlete, you're also a potential business owner, brand builder, and negotiator.

This hybrid identity is a game-changer. It gives you a unique opportunity to take control of your future beyond sports. You are gaining skills that many entrepreneurs spend years learning: to manage time under pressure, to build relationships with fans and sponsors, to negotiate contracts, and to handle money responsibly. These experiences don't just help you succeed as an athlete, they set you up to thrive in business and life.

But with this opportunity comes responsibility. You have to protect your brand, make wise financial decisions, and understand the legal side of business deals. This book will guide you through those challenges, empowering you to make choices that safeguard your eligibility and reputation while maximizing your financial and professional growth.

This is your moment. By owning your hybrid role as athlete and entrepreneur, and learning the legal and financial aspects of college sports, you are creating a solid foundation that you can use to build the life you want, not just in the present moment, but well into the future. You owe it to your 50-year-old self to attain the knowledge that will maximize your financial portfolio in those later years. That starts with learning the law that controls NIL and Rev-Share deals, and then becoming financially literate with respect to business operations and investments.

Workshop: Practical Preparation

This book is just the beginning: a foundation to build your knowledge and confidence about NIL, revenue sharing, business setup, branding, taxes, and investments. Real growth happens when you take what you've learned and put it into action. While this book stands as a valuable resource on its own, the Hopkins Law Sports Management team also offers a hands-on workshop that turns these concepts into practical steps. During an interactive presentation -- where athletes, parents, and school administrators are encouraged to ask questions -- we'll dive into the law of NIL and Rev-Share, how to start and run a successful business, and taxes and investments. Afterward, those ready to take the next step can attend the workshop to put pen to paper and start creating.

During the workshop, you'll get step-by-step guidance on setting up crucial parts of your entrepreneurial journey. Whether you want to apply for your federal Employer Identification Number (EIN), open a retirement or investment account, or have detailed questions about NIL contracts answered, you'll get direct help tailored to your needs.

This is your chance to move beyond theory and handle these important tasks with professional support. We'll walk through the paperwork, online applications, and business considerations together, so you leave the session having made real progress toward securing your financial and legal foundation.

The workshop also provides a space to ask specific questions about your own NIL or Rev-Share opportunities. No question is too big or small -- this is about empowering you to make informed decisions and avoid costly mistakes.

HOP LAW Insight: **Knowledge alone isn't enough. Success comes from taking deliberate action. The materials in this book are designed to empower you to take those first steps confidently. My goal is to turn the opportunities the new laws in college sports provide to you into lasting advantages for your future on and off the field.**

MODULE TWO

UNDERSTANDING THE LEGAL JOURNEY TO NIL & REV- SHARE

You wake up to a DM from a local brand, a text from a "collective," and an email from your school -- three offers, three rulebooks. The brand wants a photo shoot and three posts next month. The collective hints that your "value goes up if you stay on the field." The school's message mentions a new Rev-Share packet and a cap you didn't know existed. Before breakfast, you're already making legal decisions: Is this real promotion or pay-for-play? Who's actually paying, your university or a private company? Does the amount make sense for your audience, and who checks that? This module meets you in that moment -- where law, policy, and opportunity collide -- and educates you on how to read the signals fast, classify the deal correctly, and empowers you to protect your rights so the money you earn is money you keep. And later, we'll show you how to make that money start working for you.

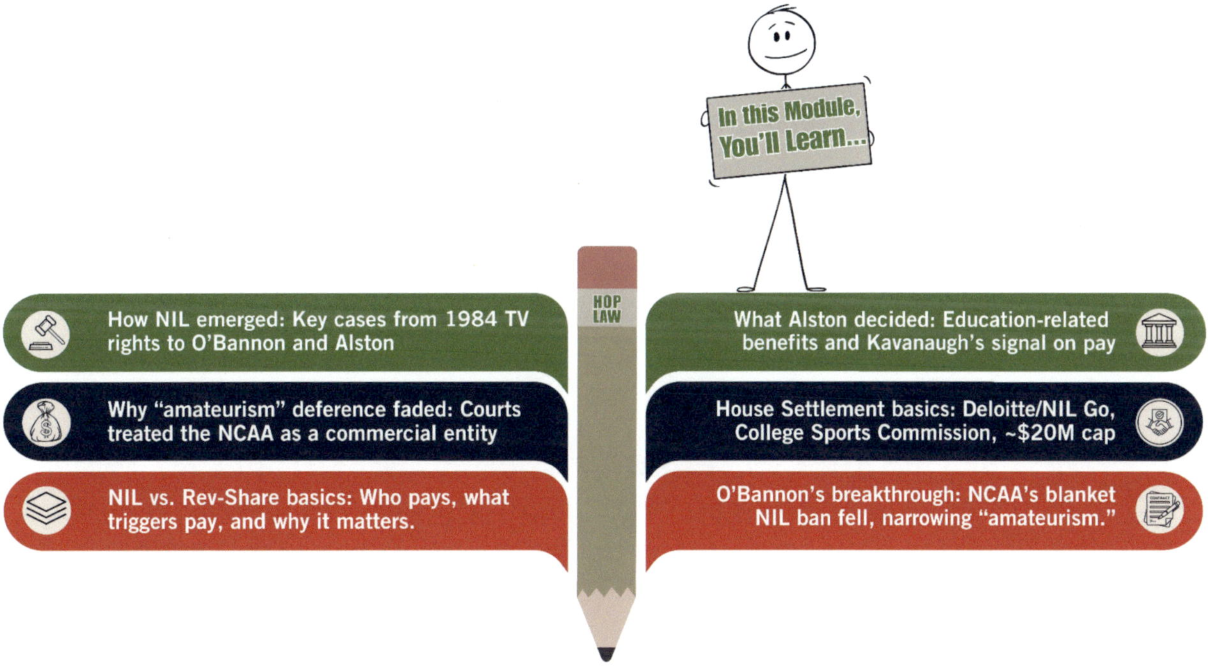

The Supreme Court's Decisions That Shaped NIL

Roadmap Highlights

- **NIL rights for college athletes emerged after decades of legal battles against the NCAA's control over athlete compensation.**

- **The NCAA historically denied athletes the right to profit from their name, image, and likeness, while schools, conferences, and media companies profited immensely.**

- **Landmark cases like *O'Bannon v. NCAA* and *NCAA v. Alston* forced the courts to recognize the NCAA's actions as commercial, removing certain protections under antitrust laws.**

- **The Supreme Court's opinion in *Alston*, particularly Justice Kavanaugh's concurring remarks, opened the door for broader athlete compensation beyond educational benefits.**

- **The 2025-26 implementation of the House Settlement formally introduces Rev-Share, allowing schools to directly pay athletes and legitimizing the NIL marketplace under regulated oversight.**

College athletes can now make money from the commercial use of their name, image, and likeness (NIL) as a result of student-athletes challenging the NCAA and proving the NCAA violated monopoly laws. It took student-athletes decades of fighting against the NCAA, but they finally got a piece of the very large revenue pie.

The NCAA, the conferences, the schools, the coaches, and the broadcast companies all get paid, and paid handsomely, because of the college players' performance and popularity. The only part of the product not getting paid was the player -- the one who the product was centered around.

Prior to 2021, the NCAA ruthlessly fought to prevent student-athletes from having property rights to, and getting paid from their name, image, and likeness. Their efforts to block any financial gain for athletes were effective, successful, and long-lasting.

How It All Started

Back in the 1970's, Alvis Waldrep, Jr., a heavily recruited high school football player, settled on TCU for his academic and athletic future. TCU awarded him a full scholarship. During a game against Alabama, Waldrep sustained an injury that left him paralyzed.

Waldrep sought medical assistance and was treated for his on-field injury. Eventually, Waldrep amassed a large number of medical bills, which he asked the university to cover. He argued that the injury occurred as a result of him playing a sport on behalf of the school. They said, no. He sued.

Bill Janscha/AP

Kent Waldrep, a former TCU running back, became a quadriplegic in 1974 when he was injured at Alabama. Waldrep helped write the Americans with Disabilities Act that passed in 1990 and has raised millions for spinal research.

It took a while; the injury happened in the 1970's but it wasn't until 2000 that the Texas Courts finally decided his case. The Texas Courts determined that student-athletes are not employees of the school, so Waldrep wasn't entitled to reimbursement for his medical expenses. *Waldrep v. Texas Employers Insurance Association*, 21 S.W.3d 692 (Tex. App. 2000).

In Waldrep's case, the judges relied on the NCAA rules that prioritized the principle of amateurism. The NCAA had strict rules against student-athletes taking pay for participation in sports. The NCAA decided that providing student-athletes with scholarships doesn't violate those rules, but paying for medical bills as a result of playing a sport does.

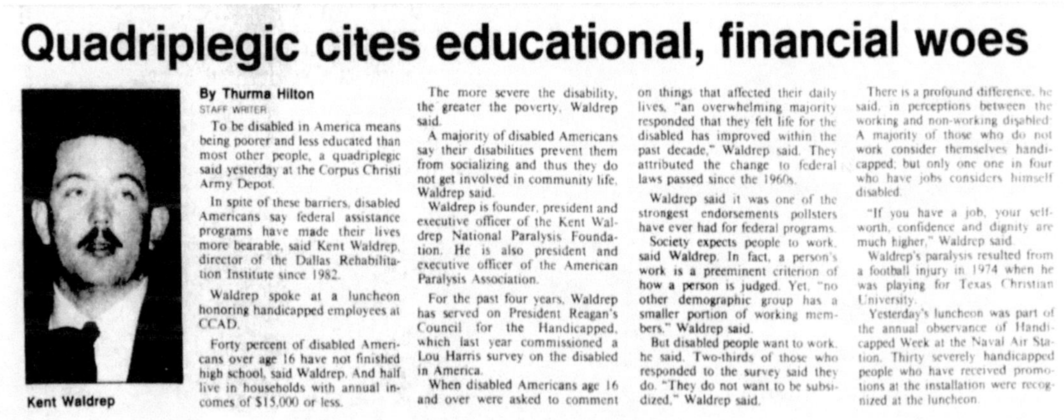

Quadriplegic cites educational, financial woes

Kent Waldrep

By Thurma Hilton
STAFF WRITER

To be disabled in America means being poorer and less educated than most other people, a quadriplegic said yesterday at the Corpus Christi Army Depot.

In spite of these barriers, disabled Americans say federal assistance programs have made their lives more bearable, said Kent Waldrep, director of the Dallas Rehabilitation Institute since 1982.

Waldrep spoke at a luncheon honoring handicapped employees at CCAD.

Forty percent of disabled Americans over age 16 have not finished high school, said Waldrep. And half live in households with annual incomes of $15,000 or less.

The more severe the disability, the greater the poverty, Waldrep said.

A majority of disabled Americans say their disabilities prevent them from socializing and thus they do not get involved in community life, Waldrep said.

Waldrep is founder, president and executive officer of the Kent Waldrep National Paralysis Foundation. He is also president and executive officer of the American Paralysis Association.

For the past four years, Waldrep has served on President Reagan's Council for the Handicapped, which last year commissioned a Lou Harris survey on the disabled in America.

When disabled Americans age 16 and over were asked to comment on things that affected their daily lives, "an overwhelming majority responded that they felt life for the disabled has improved within the past decade," Waldrep said. They attributed the change to federal laws passed since the 1960s.

Waldrep said it was one of the strongest endorsements pollsters have ever had for federal programs.

Society expects people to work, said Waldrep. In fact, a person's work is a preeminent criterion of how a person is judged. Yet, "no other demographic group has a smaller portion of working members," Waldrep said.

But disabled people want to work, he said. Two-thirds of those who responded to the survey said they do. "They do not want to be subsidized," Waldrep said.

There is a profound difference, he said, in perceptions between the working and non-working disabled: A majority of those who do not work consider themselves handicapped; but only one one in four who have jobs considers himself disabled.

"If you have a job, your self-worth, confidence and dignity are much higher," Waldrep said.

Waldrep's paralysis resulted from a football injury in 1974 when he was playing for Texas Christian University.

Yesterday's luncheon was part of the annual observance of Handicapped Week at the Naval Air Station. Thirty severely handicapped people who have received promotions at the installation were recognized at the luncheon.

Previously, the NCAA rules specifically barred athletes from making money off of their names, images, or likenesses. Those same rules didn't apply to the athletes' schools, teams, or conferences. Those institutions weren't restricted by that amateurism principle. They all capitalized not only on the popularity of a particular team but also on individual athletes and made billions of dollars in the process.

Some people say this arrangement upheld the sanctity of college athletics. But what does that mean? Sanctity means holiness or sacredness. Was it because kids played for the team they always dreamed of playing for, and, because of unfair transfer rules, were stuck with the team for four years? Did that make college football sacred? Because it was still a billion-dollar industry then like it is now.

Maybe the transfer portal reduced the piousness of the sport. Is college football less sacred because athletes are now able to seek a better opportunity elsewhere? Or, should a school have all future property rights in an athlete once they commit to a school?

There was a time where college athletes would lose a year of eligibility if they transferred schools. That rule was nonsensical. There was no basis for the rule other than to force a student to stay with the team they first picked.

All the power was with the NCAA and schools: they sold tickets, broadcasted the games, sold television rights, and made billions. They didn't choose to put the local game on the public broadcast station (PBS). They sold the most popular athletes' jerseys and collected on those sales. They licensed the players' image and likeness to video game makers and made even more money. It was a constant cash grab for the NCAA, universities, coaches, video game makers; everyone except the players.

They treated the athletes like professionals but insisted they were amateurs. And it could've all been avoided if it weren't for the NCAA's greed.

Ed O'Bannon Lawsuit

In the case of Ed O'Bannon et al., the student-athletes asked for a small share of the money if the NCAA and EA Sports were going to use their likeness in video games. The NCAA, of course, fought against that request.

Had the NCAA allowed EA Sports to pay the athletes a nominal amount, say $1,000, then we probably would have avoided the complete disaster of pay-for-play NIL deals in college sports.

Let's take it back to 1984. At that time, the United States Supreme Court decided a case brought by the University of Oklahoma and the University of Georgia against the NCAA. The NCAA mandated all schools to only contract with ABC and CBS to broadcast their games. They did this because the NCAA worked with ABC and CBS to limit the amount of games that could be broadcast so that ticket sales wouldn't take a hit to local games. The NCAA essentially rigged it so that more people would be forced to buy tickets to games if they wanted to watch their local team play.

The Universities of Oklahoma and Georgia entered into a separate deal with NBC that would allow for more televised games and greater revenues for the schools. The NCAA then announced it would take disciplinary action against any school that entered into the deal Oklahoma and Georgia made with NBC as opposed to the deal the NCAA made with ABC and CBS. Oklahoma and Georgia sued the NCAA arguing the NCAA created a monopoly by restricting how the universities could earn money.

The case made its way to the US Supreme Court, and the Court decided against the NCAA. The Supreme Court found that the NCAA violated the Sherman Act, the law that prevents monopolies in business, by the NCAA being in complete control of the broadcast rights of the college football games. The Court found that the NCAA was attempting to artificially increase the value of live tickets by restricting the universities from entering into their own deals with other television stations.

But even in that ruling, a couple of the Supreme Court justices said the NCAA shouldn't necessarily be treated like a purely commercial and profit-oriented organization. Courts historically gave the NCAA leeway when it came to antitrust regulations (monopoly laws) because the NCAA is uniquely linked to both amateur athletics and higher education. In other words, the NCAA could get away with restrictions and policies that would normally be condemned as monopolistic practices in a purely business environment.

The Court highlighted that the NCAA's position "reflects the NCAA's fundamental policy of preserving amateurism and integrating athletics and education." That finding seems to ignore how the NCAA was intentionally limiting broadcasting in order to drive up ticket sales. That practice is a strategic business decision to optimize revenue and has nothing to do with "preserving amateurism."

That case happened in 1984. Then we get to the Ed O'Bannon case in 2012. O'Bannon and other athletes wanted to be paid for EA Sports, a NCAA-licensed product, using their image and likeness in a video game. The NCAA fought against that request, too.

Had the NCAA taken the position that if a company is going to make a stand-alone product, such as a video game, they have to pay the player a regulated, nominal amount of money, then players would've only been able to be paid for video games and similar products, and paid at that certain amount. This is what the NCAA is trying to implement now under the new House Settlement rules: where athletes have to prove that the money they are receiving in NIL deals is actually tied to the promotion of a service or product.

Had the NCAA created such rules for stand-alone products, the idea of amateurism would've prevailed in later lawsuits. Courts would have drawn a distinction between a stand-alone product like video games, compared to what the unregulated NIL market is now where the actual use of the player's NIL is afterthought and the money is used solely to build out a roster.

The dollar amount being paid to the athlete -- not the product or service using their NIL -- is used to lure an athlete to a particular school. The student gets to the school and forgets they have to do the commercial they were "paid" to do; the athlete is only concerned about the NIL money, not the "job" that comes with that NIL money. And remember, the "job" isn't playing the sport, it's doing a commercial for a product.

By the NCAA fighting against Ed O'Bannon, the Court's were forced to analyze whether the NCAA was violating the monopoly laws again. The court found the NCAA was engaging in more monopolistic behavior by restricting the players' ability to be paid by a third-party for the players' NIL.

NIL *Timeline*

HOPKINS LAW SPORTS MANAGEMENT

NCAA V. NBC

1984

- NCAA violated antitrust laws by artificially inflating ticket prices.
- The Supreme Court started to doubt whether NCAA was only about amateur sports and education.

O'BANNON V. NCAA

2012

- NCAA refused to let athletes be paid for their NIL in video games.
- Courts ruled the NCAA was acting as a business, violating monopoly laws — opening the door for future lawsuits.

NCAA V. ALSTON

2021

- SCOTUS ruled the NCAA couldn't block education-related benefits.
- Kavanaugh warned NCAA rules on athlete pay likely violate antitrust law.
- NCAA changed its compensation rules 10 days later & "NIL" deals became the norm.

HOUSE SETTLEMENT

2024

- New rules restrict NIL deals and allow third-party oversight.
- Colleges can now pay athletes directly through revenue sharing.
- Each D-I school has a $20M salary cap to divide as they choose.

HOPKINS LAW
EDUCATED & EMPOWERED ATHLETES

The court decided that the NCAA's amateurism rules were no longer valid. The court came to that decision because of the way the NCAA operates: more as a commercial enterprise rather than one regulating amateur student-athletes. Therefore, the court decided that the NCAA regulations can now be held to the typical standard under monopoly laws. The court also found that the players established that they suffered an injury. The injury was that if it weren't for the NCAA rules that prevented athletes from being paid, EA Sports would have likely paid the college athletes for the right to use their names, images, and likenesses in video games.

The O'Bannon case decided the major issue that the NCAA's actions -- how they conduct business -- is commercial activity, not rules just governing amateur athletics and higher education. With the Supreme Court's determination that the NCAA engages in commercial activity rather than amateur athletics, they are now subject to additional scrutiny under monopoly laws.

Following the O'Bannon decision, the door opened for more lawsuits and several players filed various lawsuits against the NCAA. One of those suits was NCAA vs. Alston.

NCAA v. Alston

In the Alston case, the student-athletes argued, among other claims, that the NCAA rules didn't allow them to receive "non-cash education-related benefits." Those benefits included things like "computers, science equipment, musical instruments and other tangible items not included in the cost of attendance calculation, but, nonetheless, related to the pursuit of academic studies."

The Alston case labeled those benefits "academic benefits." The Supreme Court decided the NCAA's rules restricting those education-related benefits for student-athletes also violate monopoly laws. It was a unanimous decision -- even Justices Thomas and Alito sided with the athletes.

Here's the mystifying part: The NCAA actually won the argument related to *non-education* payments to students (NIL payments). Those are the payments currently happening when a student receives money from an NIL deal, such as Bryce Underwood getting paid over $12 million to play for the University of Michigan. That's a non-education payment because it has nothing to do with the student-athlete's education, whereas payments for computers or science equipment is an education-related benefit. The Alston case was about payments and benefits related to academic issues, or education-related benefits.

Even though the student-athletes lost the non-education payments argument (NIL), here's how and why the NCAA agreed to change the rules that allow those payments.

A bit of court procedure is required to understand what happened: A case has to go through two other courts before the Supreme Court hears it. The first court is called the district court. After the district court decides a case, the case gets appealed to what is called the court of appeals. In this case, the case was appealed to the Ninth Circuit Court of Appeals.

In the Alston case, the Ninth Circuit Court of Appeals decided that the NCAA has a legitimate interest in "preserving amateurism" when it comes to paying players (this is the non-education payments). So the NCAA defeated the student-athletes' request to get paid under NIL deals (non-education related payments). The students didn't appeal that issue to the Supreme Court - they were content on not pursuing non-education related payments. They only appealed the decision denying them education-related benefits, such as computers.

And because the student-athletes who brought the lawsuit didn't appeal the Ninth Circuit's ruling upholding the NCAA's rules relating to students receiving money that is "untethered to education," the Supreme Court didn't actually rule on that aspect of the case. But that's the aspect of the case that is currently allowing student athletes to get paid for non-education benefits, such as commercials, being gifted cars, and other NIL deals.

Here's how it happened.

The sentence that changed college athlete compensation:

"There are serious questions whether the NCAA's remaining compensation rules can pass muster under ordinary rule of reason scrutiny."

—Justice Kavanaugh

In issuing the ruling, Justice Kavanaugh first acknowledged that the student-athletes didn't appeal the issue of non-education payments (things unrelated to academics). He understood that the Supreme Court was only deciding whether student athletes could receive benefits related to academics -- those things like computers or musical instruments.

He then fired a shot heard 'round the college sports world. He surmised, "there are serious questions whether the NCAA's remaining compensation rules can pass muster under ordinary rule of reason scrutiny."

By writing that one sentence, Kavanaugh tipped the Supreme Court's hand and let the NCAA know that if student-athletes were to bring a case back to the Supreme Court relating to compensation for non-academic activities, the athletes would win. The Supreme Court would strike down any NCAA rules restricting athlete compensation as a violation of monopoly laws.

Technically, what Justice Kavanaugh wrote was not binding because the players didn't appeal that issue (non-academic benefits); he just gave his opinion, and likely the entire Supreme Court's opinion, on the issue. By doing that, he let the NCAA know that their rules against player compensation are also violating monopoly laws.

Justice Kavanaugh made that statement in the Alston case on June 21, 2021. The NCAA changed the compensation rules ten days later.

THE FINE PRINT:
From "Amateurism" to Pay - What Changed

HOW THE NCAA RESTRICTED PAY:

- For decades, NCAA rules banned athlete compensation, claiming these limits preserved "amateurism," protected competitive balance, and maintained consumer demand (fans preferred the "amateur" model of college sports).
- Courts gave the NCAA deference under antitrust law (said it was okay to not pay athletes because of the amateur justification).

HOW THE NCAA LOST:

- Over time, Courts increasingly viewed the NCAA as a commercial business, so they would need to justify restraining pay just as any other business would.
- In Alston, SCOTUS unanimously applied the rule of reason ("amateurism" isn't a free pass anymore, the NCAA has to justify not paying athletes) and removed the NCAA's limits on education-related benefits, and (via Kavanaugh's concurrence) signaled that a cap on non-education-related benefits (pay) would likely fail. The NCAA changed the pay rule 10 days after SCOTUS decided Alston.
- Facing continued antitrust pressure, the NCAA settled the House case. The House Settlement allows athletes to get paid in two ways: Rev-Share (schools pay) and NIL (athird party pays).

The Alston case essentially means that the NCAA, by being in full control of the NIL and not paying any athlete for any use of their name, image, or likeness (and not permitting any other company to pay a student-athlete for their NIL), is, again, breaking monopoly laws, and has been for decades.

So up until the O'Bannon case, the NCAA had long argued -- and argued successfully -- that monopoly laws actually permitted them to restrict athlete compensation or not allow the athletes to get paid. The reasoning behind that argument was the NCAA was promoting competitive equity among teams and distinguishing college athletics from professional sports. That is, the NCAA was promoting amateurism. The O'Bannon court determined that to be a lie.

The Alston Court then decided that the NCAA would be subject to regular monopoly laws because it's operating as a commercial enterprise. In other words, the NCAA and college sports are seen by the Supreme Court as a regular business, like Amazon or Nike. The Alston case expressly decided that student-athletes can get education-related benefits (computers, etc.), and Justice Kavanaugh directed, off the record, that the athletes can be paid for non-education benefits, like car commercials. That's how we got to this version of NIL.

Beginning in 2021, with the new NIL rules, the NIL landscape has resembled the Wild West. Essentially, there are no real rules. It's the Napster or LimeWire era of college sports. The consensus among all involved in college sports, however, is that rules are desperately needed in the NIL arena.

As a result of more lawsuits, those rules are now set to be implemented in the 2025-26 academic year. There were three class-action lawsuits brought by student-athletes against the NCAA. The students made various legal claims relating to being paid in one way or another, and out of those lawsuits, the NCAA and athletes have entered into a settlement called the House Settlement. House is the name of one of the athletes suing the NCAA.

The House Settlement created a long, detailed list of rules for college sports. One of those new rules allows the NCAA to oversee NIL deals by placing certain rules and restrictions on the deals. The goal of those restrictions is to legitimize the NIL market among college athletes and not use NIL money to build out rosters. So now, there are specific rules businesses must follow in order to pay an athlete for use of their NIL. If those rules are violated, then the deals will be canceled. That oversight is being handled by a third party, not the NCAA.

The most significant aspect of the House Settlement, however, is that universities are now allowed to pay their student-athletes directly for their participation in a sport. That's called

Rev-Share. The college athletes now receive a share of the revenue generated from college sports. It's legal for a college to pay a student to play a sport.

The House Settlement allocates $20.5 million to each Division I school to pay student-athletes. That's the college salary cap. The settlement doesn't have any set rules on how the school has to distribute the $20.5 million to the athletes. An equal split of the money is not required and schools are free to divvy up the money as they see fit among their athletic programs.

So that's how we got to where we are now with college students getting paid to play sports. It all started with a severely injured TCU football player asking to have medical bills covered, to O'Bannon asking for a little money for his likeness in a video game, to Bryce Underwood getting paid $12 million. That escalated quickly.

More lawsuits are pending and more will be filed until this all works itself out. For now, get ready to hear about college athletes signing multi-year deals for more money that some people will make in a lifetime. Even if you aren't signing a major deal worth millions, it's still important to take the correct legal and financial steps to protect yourself, your assets, and maximize your earnings.

House Settlement Brings Rev-Share & NIL Rules

The House case didn't appear out of thin air. It's the inevitable result of decades of the NCAA treating college sports like a business while insisting the athletes aren't part of the business model. College athletes -- full grown adults -- often spending full-time hours at practices, meetings, working out, games, travel, and film study, have been historically told to be grateful for the opportunity to play a sport for their university. The narrative was college sports are amateur sports and amateurs don't deserve to be paid. Meanwhile, every other person and entity exploited college sports for every dollar they could get, to the tune of billions. The school didn't have to pay the football coach a $100,000,000 million contract -- the math teacher could get a small stipend to coach; the SEC didn't have to enter the multi-billion (with a "b") dollar contract with ESPN/Disney -- PBS could air the local game; and the list goes on.

But the masses were conditioned to think that of all the figures in college sports, the adults who are the foundation of it all should receive the least. If all the other adults are going to exploit college sports -- that is, remove all remnants of it being anything resembling amateur sports -- then the adults who work the hardest and put themselves at physical risk (yes, knowingly and willingly) should also get paid. At least, that's what the United States

Supreme Court has reasoned (after numerous cases where SCOTUS warned the adults to stop exploiting college sports).

One of those cases was the O'Bannon case. And after *O'Bannon* cracked open the door on commercial rights and *Alston* pushed the NCAA under ordinary antitrust scrutiny (instead of the NCAA avoiding monopoly liability because of "amateur status"), the class actions bundled under *House v. NCAA* took the next step: if your industry runs on athletes' labor and their commercial value, the athletes deserve a lawful share of the revenue -- and any rules that suppress that value should be judged like any other restraint in a commercial market. The House litigation challenged long-standing compensation limits and the way NIL was effectively used (or restricted) across the system. Rather than risk a definitive, potentially sweeping trial result, the parties negotiated a comprehensive settlement that doesn't end the conversation, but does finally write athlete compensation into the rulebook.

With court approval of the House settlement, we have entered a new era of college sports. Universities can now directly pay student-athletes ("Rev-Share"), and athletes can enter into NIL deals with third parties.

Over the past few years, it's felt like there were no rules when it came to paying athletes; whichever schools could scrape together the most money

HOUSE V. NCAA *Explained*

HOPKINS LAW SPORTS MANAGEMENT

WHAT IT IS:

- A **class-action antitrust case** brought by college athletes challenging NCAA limits on athlete compensation.
- The parties reached a global agreement known as the **House Settlement.**

ATHLETES CLAIMED:

- NCAA rules unlawfully restricted athlete pay and suppressed NIL value.
- Athletes were entitled to compensation tied to the commercial revenues their play generates.

SETTLEMENT TERMS:

- **Revenue Sharing (Rev-Share):** Schools may pay athletes directly from athletics revenues, subject to an annual school cap ($20.5M for D-I at launch, 4% increase each year afterwards).
- **NIL Oversight:** Third-party review of all significant NIL deals to ensure a valid business purpose and fair-market value (no pay-for-play).
- **New Enforcement:** A College Sports Commission oversees compliance; decisions can go to neutral arbitration.
- **Coexistence:** Rev-Share (school pays you to play) sits alongside NIL (third parties pay for real promotion/licensing).

WHY IT MATTERS:

- This formalizes athlete pay within clear rules, moving college sports from "anything goes" toward **regulated, enforceable compensation.**

HLOSPORTS.COM

were the most competitive. These new rules are designed to level that playing field if followed by the schools (and that's one big "if").

That "if" is doing a lot of work. The settlement attempts to channel money through two lawful lanes: Rev-Share, where the school pays you under a contract that looks and feels like a real compensation agreement; and NIL, where third parties pay you for a true commercial purpose -- promotion, endorsement, appearances, or licensing -- at fair-market rates, with actual deliverables. The idea is simple: if a school is paying you to participate, that's Rev-Share. If a brand is paying you to promote, that's NIL. Mixing the two -- like a third party paying you purely to enroll at a particular school -- lands you back in the old, illegal pay-for-play territory the settlement is trying to shut down.

There are terms in the House settlement that allow for the creation of a couple of entities to oversee the payments received by athletes, one for NIL deals and one for rev-share agreements.

First, Deloitte will oversee the third-party NIL payments. These are not the payments made by the universities to the players. These are payments made by private parties, including the collectives, to the college athletes.

What does that mean in practice? Any significant NIL agreement (including deals arranged by collectives) must be submitted to a centralized clearinghouse. Deloitte's role is to check whether there's a valid business purpose (real marketing or licensing tied to goods or services sold to the public), clear deliverables and timelines, and compensation that's commensurate with fair market value. If the money exists just to stack a roster -- no ads, no appearances, no content, no licensing -- that's a problem. If the rate is wildly out of line with comparable non-student creators, that's a problem. Deloitte can request more information, push back on terms, or refuse to clear a deal that looks like disguised pay-for-play. This process won't make every judgment perfect, but it creates a paper trail and a standard that never existed before.

Second, the College Sports Commission, a newly formed entity, will oversee the athletes and schools' compliance with all aspects of the settlement, including rev-share agreements. The Commission is essentially the new NCAA enforcement entity. It will implement investigations into all aspects of paying players, and it will make decisions based on the investigations, including issuing penalties against players and schools.

Think of the Commission as the on-field referee for Rev-Share and the broader settlement rules. Schools that opt in to Rev-Share will have an annual compensation cap to manage across their rosters. The Commission monitors how schools structure those agreements: term lengths, payment schedules, redshirt treatment, performance incentives (athletic and academic), buyout provisions, and reporting. If a school tries to sneak around the cap, uses conditional scholarship threats, or retaliates for a redshirt request by cutting guaranteed pay with no contractual basis, the Commission can step in. This is where we'll likely see the earliest case law outcomes: is a clause enforceable? Is a termination justified? Does a "redshirt reduction" clause violate the rule that Rev-Share isn't pay-for-play?

The House settlement allows players, schools, and conferences the ability to have the decisions made by either Deloitte or the Commission reviewed by an arbitrator, and ultimately a judge, if they disagree with a decision from either entity.

That appeals ladder matters. In the NIL lane, if Deloitte flags a deal as non-compliant, the athlete or payor can contest it with more evidence -- engagement metrics, comparable market rates, refined deliverables. In the Rev-Share lane, if the Commission sanctions a school or withholds approval for a contract structure, the parties can push for arbitration and, if necessary, court review. That's transparency and due process that didn't exist when everything was being handled informally or in the shadows.

The new regulatory framework for college sports simply broke the NCAA up into a couple more entities. There's still oversight of the colleges, players, and all others associated with college sports; the difference is now the players are being legitimately paid and the rules are completely new. Because of the newness of everything, there's a ton of wrinkles that will need to be ironed out. I suspect most of that ironing will be done in court.

Here are a few of those wrinkles (places where the rules will meet real life):

- ❖ **Rev-Share caps and roster strategy:** Each Division I school has an annual Rev-Share cap to distribute. There's no requirement to split it equally. Expect creative compensation structures: multi-year stability clauses, academic bonuses, and performance incentives. Expect disputes, too (especially around redshirting, medical hardships, and mid-season coaching changes).

- ❖ **The collective question:** Collectives aren't disappearing. Under a compliant NIL model, they must function like real marketers or licensors, not payroll departments. That means documented campaigns, appearances, content calendars, and rates tied to true market value. Deals that used to say "$X if you enroll here" now need actual ads and deliverables that justify paying athletes.

- **No more "wink-and-nod" deals:** The combination of Deloitte review, school reporting, and Commission oversight is designed to squeeze out "phantom work" and enrollment-contingent terms. If a clause says compensation stops the moment you transfer or request a redshirt -- without any business-purpose rationale -- you'll have leverage to challenge it.

- **School IP and marks:** Your NIL rights are yours. The school's trademarks are the school's. If a brand wants you in official gear or on-field imagery, that's a separate license. Expect more three-party coordination: athlete, brand/collective, and school licensing.

- **State law and conference overlays:** The settlement doesn't erase state statutes or conference policy. You still have to navigate layers that may impose notice rules, agent licensing requirements, or category restrictions.

- **Documentation culture:** NIL and Rev-Share both create a new habit for athletes: save everything. Contracts, addenda, deliverable logs, screenshots of posts, appearance sign-ins, analytics, and correspondence. If a payment is withheld or a deal is challenged, your file is your protection.

Where does this leave you? In a world with two legitimate pay channels and real accountability. The House framework won't magically stop bad behavior, but it gives you tools to insist on clean contracts, to separate playing compensation from promotional compensation, and to appeal when gatekeepers get it wrong. Most importantly, it recognizes, in black and white, what the courts have been signaling for years: college sports operate like a business, and the athletes belong in the compensation conversation -- openly, transparently, and with enforceable rights.

MODULE THREE

MASTERING THE ESSENTIALS OF NIL LAW, DEALS, & COMPLIANCE

NIL is your legal right to earn from your identity -- your name, your image, your likeness -- through real business deals, not pay-for-play. This module turns the headlines you hear about into a practical playbook: what qualifies as a compliant deal, how to price your value, how to read (and negotiate) contracts, how oversight works under House, and how to protect your eligibility while building a brand that lasts beyond college. We'll get to all of those concepts throughout this book, but for now, let's focus on NIL.

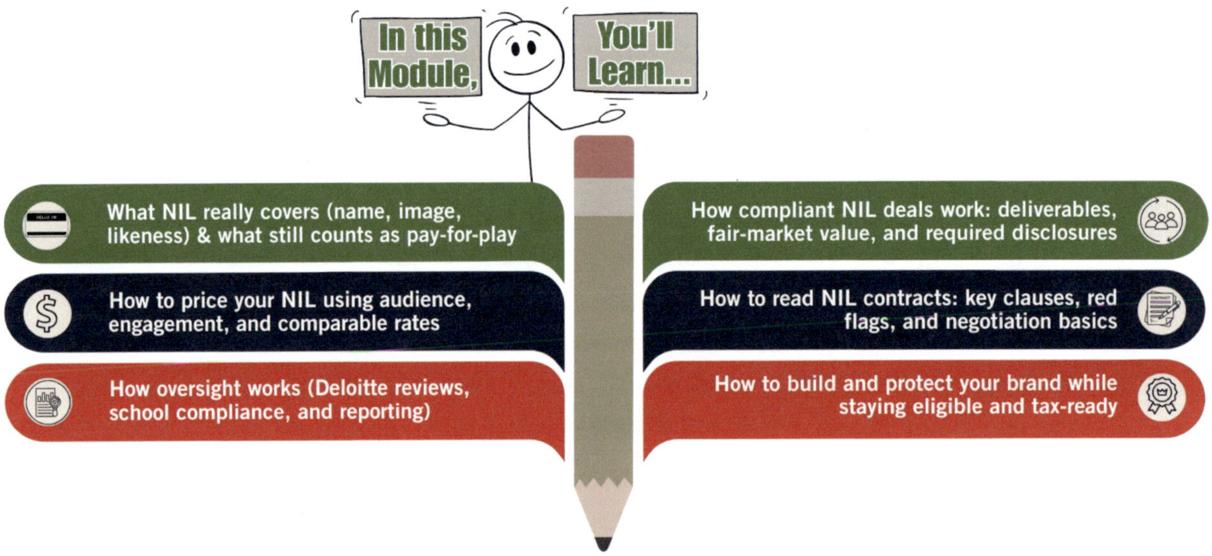

What is NIL? (Name, Image, and Likeness)

NIL stands for Name, Image, and Likeness -- the rights you have as a college athlete to profit from your own personal brand. For decades, college athletes were barred from earning money beyond their scholarships. That all changed in 2021 when the NCAA lifted restrictions and opened the door for athletes like you to monetize your name, your image, and the way you are recognized by fans and companies.

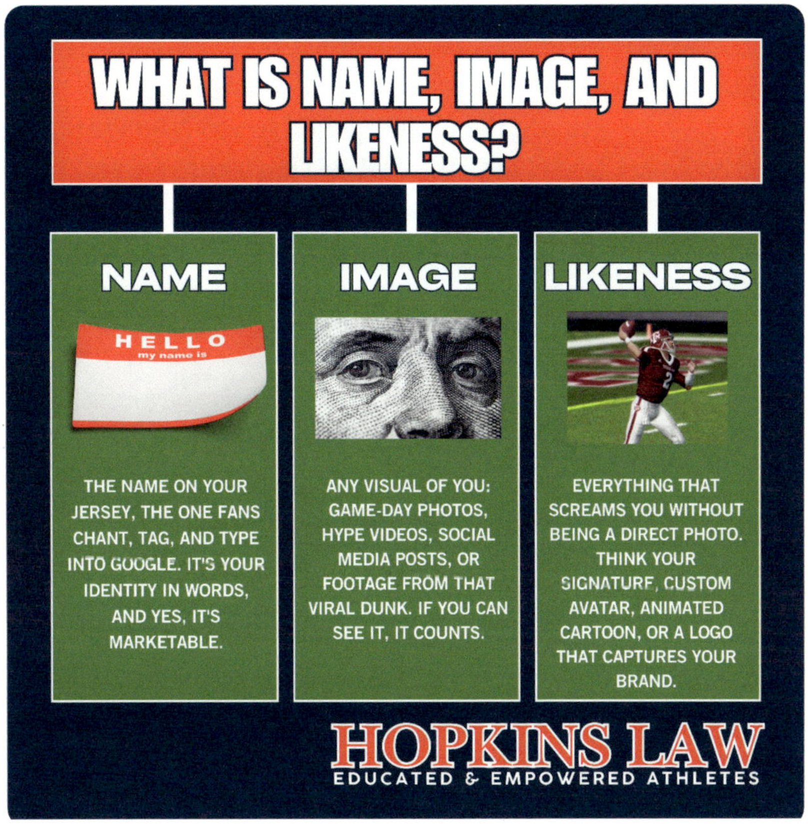

Thanks to NIL, you can now sign endorsement deals, earn money from sponsorships, make paid public appearances, promote products on your social channels, and even start your own business ventures under your brand -- all while maintaining your college eligibility.

This shift is historic because it recognizes the value you bring. The colleges, conferences, and NCAA have made billions by showcasing your talent and hard work for years. Now, you have the power to share in the rewards and take control of your future.

NIL is more than just a way to earn money during college. It's your opportunity to build a lasting personal brand, develop business skills, and create financial security that goes beyond sports.

However, it also comes with responsibilities. Knowing your rights, understanding contracts, and managing your earnings wisely are crucial to protecting your eligibility, reputation, and long-term success.

This book is here to help you navigate those opportunities and challenges. Understanding NIL is the first step toward not just making money, but making smart decisions that fuel your growth as both an athlete and entrepreneur.

What NIL Really Means (In Practice)

NIL is your legal right to be paid for promoting or licensing your identity -- your name, your photos/video, and anything that clearly points to you (signature, avatar, logo). It is NOT pay-for-play. Every legitimate NIL deal ties payment to a real business purpose (ads, appearances, content, licensing) at a fair market rate. Here's a breakdown of what is and what isn't allowed:

What's Allowed (Typical Examples)

- Sponsored posts, brand ambassadorships, paid appearances.
- Licensing your NIL for trading cards, video games, or merch.
- Creator monetization (YouTube/podcasts), personal training, camps/clinics.
- Your own products (apparel, gear, etc.), paid speaking.

What's Not Allowed / High Risk

- Payment contingent on enrolling at or staying with a specific school.
- "Deals" with no deliverables or business purpose (pure roster-building).
- Overbroad, perpetual rights to your NIL that you can't revoke.
- Using school marks/logos without permission (separate license needed).

Payment Under NIL Agreements

As mentioned above, the House settlement allows for college athletes to receive payments from either third parties or the school they attend.

Payments to college athletes will be in two forms, 1) NIL deals that have been happening for the past few years, and 2) new payments under the revenue-sharing (Rev-Share) model created by the House settlement. The players and NCAA agreed, as part of the House settlement, that NIL deals will now have rules that must be followed to ensure the payments to the athletes are legitimate.

The specific language in the House settlement is as follows:

Prevents "Boosters" (individually or in a collective) from entering into NIL licenses with or for the benefit of current or prospective student-athletes unless:

1. **The license/payment is for a valid business purpose related to the promotion or endorsement of goods or services provided to the general public for profit;**

2. **The compensation rates and terms must be commensurate with compensation paid to similarly-situated individuals with comparable NIL value;**
3. **Those comparable individuals can't be current or prospective student-athletes at the Member Institution.**

The NCAA or Conference has to provide for neutral arbitration if there's proposed discipline for a Member Institution or student-athlete violating these rules.

The new rule requires the payment to the athlete to be linked to a valid business purpose, and that business purpose must be related to the promotion or endorsement of goods or services.

Previous NIL deals were almost exclusively conditioned on a player playing for a particular school, not for the endorsement of a good or service. For example, the $12 million paid to Bryce Underwood to enroll in the University of Michigan was paid by a billionaire whose wife was a Michigan grad and wanted to have the best quarterback at her school. It's highly unlikely Underwood promoted the billionaire's software company.

The new rule also requires that the good or service that's being promoted is provided to the general public for profit. In the past, NIL collectives were entities, sometimes just made up of a couple of people, who pooled money together to pay athletes to attend the school they were supporting. Those payments weren't tied to the player being in a commercial or any other promotional activity, and the collectives weren't selling a product or service that was available to the general public for profit.

Technically, NIL deals of the past are illegal under the new House rules. But collectives aren't going away, and illegally paying college athletes money has never and will never stop. But one firm, Deloitte, is supposed to be the watchdog of NIL deals moving forward.

All new NIL deals must be submitted to the accounting firm, Deloitte. Deloitte is serving as the clearinghouse for the NCAA with respect to all NIL deals. Deloitte will review the deals and either clear them or request additional information so they can make a final determination as to whether the deal is legitimate or not.

The Role of Collectives in NIL Deals

Collectives range from officially affiliated booster clubs to informal groups of alumni or fans pooling resources. Their sole mission: to pay athletes to play for their favorite programs. Take Bryce Underwood's $12 million move to Michigan. That money didn't come from the University of Michigan's coffers -- it was brokered by the Champions Circle NIL Collective, funded by Larry Ellison through a personal connection. This is a key distinction: these NIL deals are paid by external organizations, not the schools themselves.

Under the original NIL framework, payments were supposed to reflect genuine branding work -- endorsements, commercials, appearances -- at market rates for your name, image, and likeness. But many deals ended up as straightforward pay-for-play agreements, with little promotional work involved.

Types of NIL Deals - Endorsements, Appearances, Merch, etc.

One of the most exciting parts for a college athlete stepping into the world of NIL is discovering the wide range of opportunities you have to earn money from your name, image, and likeness. It's not just about traditional endorsements anymore, there are creative and varied ways to monetize your personal brand, connect with fans, and build lasting streams of income. This section will dive deep into the different types of NIL deals you can pursue, along with some innovative ideas to spark your entrepreneurial spirit.

1. Endorsements and Sponsorships

The classic NIL opportunity is endorsement deals where an athlete partners with businesses to promote their products or services. These can range from local companies looking to build community connections, to regional brands, all the way up to national or global corporations. You might post sponsored content on your social media, wear branded gear during public events, or be featured in marketing campaigns.

Examples: Athletic apparel companies, nutritional supplements, local restaurants, fitness centers, sports equipment brands, clothing lines.

HOP LAW Insight: **Align with brands that reflect your values and personal brand to keep authenticity. That authenticity will make you feel more fulfilled working with brands and will resonate with your supporters.**

2. Paid Appearances and Speaking Engagements

Many businesses, schools, or community organizations pay athletes to appear at events, host meet-and-greets, or speak to groups. These deals leverage your status as a recognized athlete to inspire or educate audiences.

Examples: Hosting youth sports camps, speaking at graduation or business events, appearing at community fundraisers.

HOP LAW Insight: **Prepare your message and presentation to offer real value beyond just your athletic fame. And remember, how you make the people you interact with feel is more important than what you offer them.**

3. Merchandising and Product Lines

Creating your own merchandise, such as branded apparel, hats, or even custom athletic gear, can be a valuable way to capitalize on your personal brand. With online platforms and print-on-demand services, the barrier to entry is lower than ever.

Examples: T-shirts with your nickname or logo, limited edition hats, signature workout gear.

HOP LAW Insight: **Focus on quality and design to make your merchandise stand out and create loyal fans. You'll also need to know how to market your products, which is the most important aspect of this type of business. If you're not dialed in on marketing, hire someone who is effective in that realm.**

4. Digital Content Monetization

If you create digital content like videos, tutorials, podcasts, or livestreams, there are ways to monetize that content directly. You can create videos that help younger athletes with their game, such as "how-to" videos that will assist them becoming a better player. Or, you can start a podcast talking about the life of an athlete.

Examples: Paid subscriptions on platforms like Patreon, exclusive training videos or behind-the-scenes footage, sponsored YouTube or TikTok videos.

HOP LAW Insight: **Build a niche audience and offer unique, valuable content. Always make sure to personalize the content that you make so that it is unique to you. Content that is more based in storytelling typically resonates with an audience because they are getting to know you.**

5. Social Media Influencer Partnerships

If you have a sizable social media following, companies may pay you for posts, stories, or product placements on platforms like Instagram, Twitter, or TikTok.

Examples: Sharing your workout routines featuring a brand's products, promoting healthy foods, or showcasing lifestyle brands.

HOP LAW Insight: **Always disclose sponsored content clearly to maintain trust with your followers. It's important to research businesses to make sure you are promoting ethical products that you would stand behind.**

6. Personal Services and Coaching

Offering skills as a personal coach or consultant can be a lucrative NIL opportunity, especially if you have expertise in your sport.

Examples: Private training sessions, online coaching programs, skill clinics, and branded off-season camps.

HOP LAW Insight: **Get certified, if required, and build a strong reputation for professionalism. It's better to look for ways that you can help younger athletes in a group setting or in a way that creates passive income. Working one-on-one with students can be time-consuming and usually ends up costing you more than you make, in the long run.**

7. Licensing Your Name, Image, and Likeness

Some athletes license their NIL rights to companies to create products or services. This means the company pays you while they handle product development, sales, and marketing.

Examples: Signing a deal for a video game appearance, a trading card company, or a sneaker collaboration.

HOP LAW Insight: **Make sure to have an attorney review any licensing contract to protect your interests when it comes to royalty amounts, usage rights, duration, and many other contractual issues.**

8. <u>Collaborations and Partnerships</u>

Join forces with other athletes, creators, or businesses to co-create products, events, or experiences.

Examples: Launching a joint apparel line with a teammate, hosting a community sports event sponsored by local businesses.

HOP LAW Insight: Collaborations are beneficial to all parties because it merges two audiences and the collaborators gain new supporters that they otherwise wouldn't have had. Always find collaborators who complement your brand and share your vision. Remember, keep it authentic!

9. <u>Scholarships and Educational Sponsorships</u>

While these don't pay you directly for NIL rights, some companies or foundations offer scholarships or educational support tied to your athletic and personal brand.

Examples: A company sponsoring your tuition in exchange for ambassador roles.

HOP LAW Insight: Weigh the value of educational support alongside cash deals.

10. <u>Creative and Emerging NIL Ideas</u>

<u>Virtual Experiences</u>: Host paid virtual Q&A sessions, game analysis, or fan chats.

<u>NFTs and Digital Collectibles</u>: Limited edition digital cards, highlights, or autographed images sold on blockchain platforms.

<u>Guest Appearances</u>: Monetize guest spots or collaborate on athlete-focused podcasts.

<u>Community Crowdfunding</u>: Launch fan-driven patronage programs where supporters contribute in exchange for exclusive perks.

There is no one-size-fits-all approach to NIL deals. Your opportunities are only limited by your creativity and goals. The best deals align with who you are as a person and athlete, enhance your brand, and set you up for long-term success.

HOP LAW Insight: Every deal you enter impacts your brand, eligibility, and financial future. Always seek advice if you're unsure, keep records, and focus on partnerships that respect your values and vision.

Key Terms Too Look For In Every NIL Deal

The world of NIL deals can seem complex and overwhelming, but understanding the key terms in every agreement is critical to protecting yourself and making confident, informed decisions. Since the *House v. NCAA* settlement introduced the new Rev-Share model, NIL deals have shifted away from pay-to-play incentives toward transparent, business-focused contracts subject to strict oversight. With the College Sports Commission, NIL Go, and the Deloitte firm overseeing any significant NIL deal, it's critical to ensure that the NIL deal you're signing is compliant.

1. The Importance of a Written Contract

The first step to compliance is a written contract. One of the most fundamental concepts with NIL agreements is that nothing should be left to informal text messages or handshake deals. Every NIL deal must be a negotiated, signed, and legally binding contract. This document clearly outlines each party's obligations, payment schedules, deliverables, and important terms, eliminating confusion and reducing risks of disputes. The introduction of NIL Go -- a centralized clearinghouse overseen by Deloitte -- ensures every NIL deal above a $600 threshold is formally reviewed for compliance.

THE FINE PRINT: Gervon Dexter v. B.L.A. Fund, II

WHO: Former University of Florida football player Gervon Dexter.

WHAT: Dexter signed an NIL deal worth $436,000 in college. In return, he owed 15% of his NFL salary for the next 25 years. Dexter was drafted in the second round and BLA requested their 15% of his contract. Dexter sued to cancel the contract.

WHAT WENT WRONG: Dexter didn't have a lawyer review his contract. Buried in the 30+ page contract was the term that he owes BLA 15% of his NFL earnings.

ISSUES: There a few issues in this case, such as BLA wasn't a registered agent in Florida, the NIL deal tied payments to future earnings and extended beyond college, and nondisclosure of the deal to Dexter's university; all of which violate Florida's NIL law.

LIKELY RESULT: While there may be a dispute as to which state law controls (Delaware or Florida), the court is likely to find that the contract terminated by operation of law (NIL deals are only valid while the athlete has college eligibility).

TAKEAWAY: Always have a lawyer review NIL contracts. Hidden or confusing terms can cost you millions, even years after college, and could require unnecessary litigation.

2. Legitimate Business Purpose and Fair Market Value

Under the House settlement, NIL deals must serve a legitimate business purpose. This means the deal must genuinely promote goods or services sold to the public for profit, rather than acting as a disguised bribe or pay-for-play incentive. Companies are required to pay fair market value, reflecting reasonable compensation based on your brand's reach, influence, and engagement.

3. Decoupling Compensation from Enrollment or Play

One of the most transformative key terms required in all NIL deals is that payment cannot be contingent on you attending or playing for a particular school. This clause breaks the old "play-for-pay" dynamic that once threatened to rig recruiting battles.

What does this mean for you? Simply put, accepting NIL compensation from a business does not mean you have to commit to or remain at a certain university. You retain your autonomy to transfer schools or make decisions about your athletic career without fear of losing NIL income.

4. The Conflict with Businesses Seeking Exclusivity

Many companies will want to include language requiring you to attend a specific school or prohibit you from working with a direct competitor (known as exclusivity clauses). They seek to maximize the value of their investment by linking payment to your enrollment or allegiance.

This raises an ongoing legal debate: do NCAA or federal courts have the authority to restrict private businesses from offering money that incentivizes where you attend? College sports stakeholders are watching developments and considering anti-tampering rules, similar to the NFL, which prohibits teams from using endorsements to influence player relocation, preserving competitive balance and athlete freedom.

In addition, no NIL deal should control your name, image, and likeness rights exclusively. You'll want to be in control over what companies you work with and how your name, image and likeness are used by those companies.

5. Future Earnings

NIL deals with college athletes are only valid so long as the athlete has college eligibility. Some businesses have attempted to (and did) include terms in NIL deals that require athletes to pay the business a portion of the money they make in a professional capacity. Those terms should be struck from every NIL deal.

6. Additional Key Contract Terms to Know

Payment Terms: Specify when and how you will be paid (lump sum, installments, bonuses).

Term of the Contract: This is how long you will be obligated to perform the tasks or "deliverables" that are listed in the contract.

Deliverables and Obligations: These are the tasks you must do in return for the money you receive from the business. These typically include social media posts, appearances, autograph signings, and appearing in commercials.

Exclusivity: As mentioned above, exclusivity clauses are designed to limit either which other companies you work for, and/or who controls the rights to your name, image, and likeness. Sometimes, non-compete clauses make sense, such as if you do a deal with Coke, they won't want you using your name, image, and likeness to promote Pepsi. Be careful of any exclusivity language, however, because sometimes it can severely limit your NIL opportunities.

Termination Clauses: Conditions under which the contract can be canceled by either party without penalty. It's always nice to give yourself an out in any contract. To do that, spell out when and how either side can end the deal, and what happens to money already paid or owed. Separate "for cause" (serious breach, no-show, fraud) from "without cause" (business change, strategy shift), and include a cure period (e.g., 10–15 days to fix a problem after written notice). Tie termination of the contract to clear, objective triggers -- not vague "harm to reputation." If there's a morals clause, narrow it to objectively verifiable conduct and require a final determination (not rumors). Add pro-rata payment for completed deliverables prior to the termination of the contract, define clawbacks only when work wasn't done, and state what survives (e.g., confidentiality, payment obligations, dispute resolution). Give yourself an easy exit if the sponsor misses payments or tries to change deliverables midstream.

Use of Image Rights: Define exactly what they can use (your name, image, voice, signature, logo), where (territory), how (media and platforms), and for how long (term + any limited sell-off window). Require pre-approval on final cuts and captions; ban edits that misrepresent you, and restrict AI/alterations without written consent. Limit exclusivity to a narrow category (e.g., "carbonated soft drinks"), set a reasonable blackout period (if any), and keep all other categories open. Prohibit sublicensing except to named partners for the specific campaign. After the term, require takedown of digital uses within a set period, allow archival use only (no new ads), and ensure school marks are cleared separately (your NIL ≠ university trademarks).

Confidentiality: Define what's confidential (rates, drafts, strategy, non-public terms) and for how long it must stay that way, with sensible carve-outs: info you must disclose to NIL Go/clearinghouse, your university compliance office, and your lawyer/CPA/agent. Permit a joint announcement with your approval on timing and wording; ban using your name in press or investor materials beyond the approved release. Include standard exceptions (already public, independently known, required by law with notice). Make it mutual, so the brand can't share your personal info or contract scans. Add a practical remedy: injunctive relief for leaks plus fee shifting if you prevail, while avoiding punitive overreach for honest, required disclosures.

Governing Law and Dispute Resolution: Specifies which laws govern the contract and how disputes will be handled. Typically, the law that governs the contract will be the state where you attend school. The contract should explicitly state this, however.

Why Understanding These Terms Matters

Informed athletes get better deals, avoid scams, and protect their eligibility and reputation. Well-drafted deals also avoid litigation (or at least provide superior protection if you are sued). Before signing any NIL contract:

- Read every word carefully. Don't sign if you don't understand something.
- Seek advice from trusted advisors: legal, financial, or compliance professionals.
- Watch for red flags like pay-for-play language or vague deliverables.
- Use the NIL Go system as your safety net to ensure compliance and transparency.

NIL was created to empower you, not to trap you. Mastering the key terms in every deal will safeguard your career and open doors to opportunity.

MODULE FOUR

LEARNING REV-SHARE RULES, PAY STRUCTURES & YOUR RIGHTS

You're sitting across from the school's General Manager at a long, mahogany wood conference table in a room full of the school's logos and large posters of the best players to attend the university. This person's position -- GM -- didn't exist just a year ago. The rules changed and now someone in a brand new position is sliding a contract that also didn't exist in college sports a year ago -- a Rev-Share agreement. It's filled with legal jargon you may be reading for the first time: pay schedule, incentives, redshirt language, a buyout clause -- this isn't simply an opportunity to make money playing the sport you love. It's a contract that could bind you to the school for your entire college career. This module will start by showing you how that money actually moves -- what counts toward the college salary cap, how schools design offers, what happens if you redshirt or enter the portal, who polices the rules, and how Rev-Share and NIL run in separate lanes so you don't step on a landmine. We'll let you review sample clauses that you'll likely find in your Rev-Share agreement. By the end, you'll know how to read the offer in your hand, spot risks, and lock in a deal that not just pays you, but more importantly, protects you.

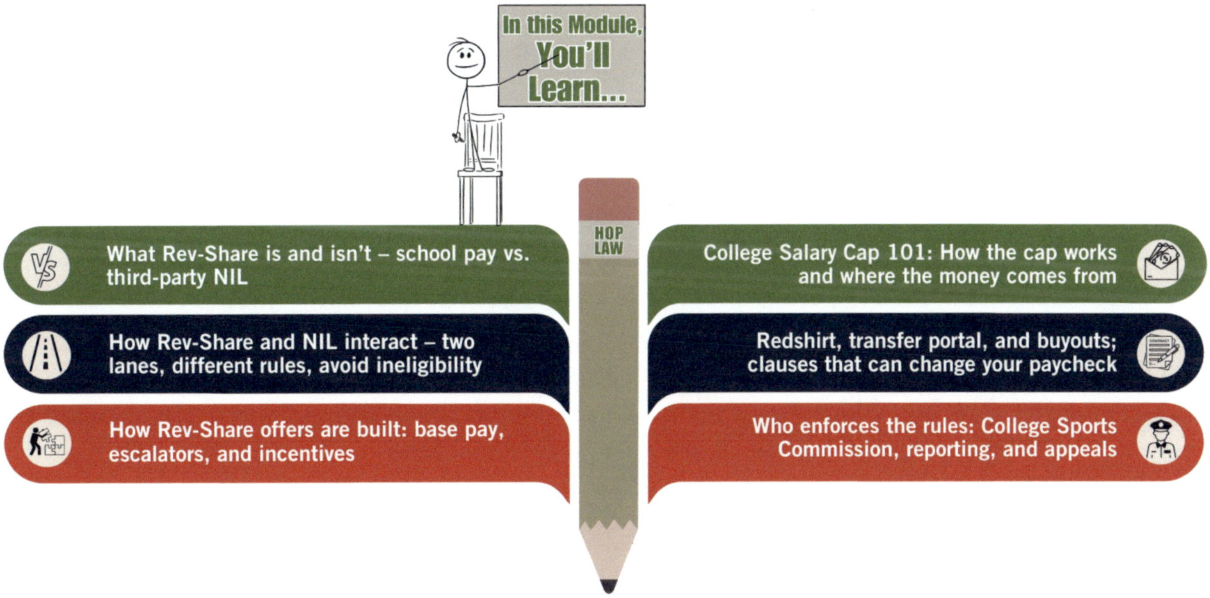

Understanding Rev-Share in College Sports

For years, people talked like schools were cutting seven-figure checks straight from university budgets to athletes. That wasn't the reality. Collectives and boosters were paying players through NIL deals, often with little structure. The House settlement finally puts direct school-to-athlete pay on the books. Rev-Share is the formal way for universities to compensate players out of the athletic department's revenue, with rules, oversight, and contracts that look a lot more like what you see in professional sports.

But what exactly does that mean?

College sports generate revenue from over twenty different streams -- including, among others, TV and media rights, ticket sales, sponsorships, merchandise, and licensing. The House Settlement allows schools to allocate a portion of eight of these revenue streams specifically to compensating athletes. This is the essence of revenue sharing (Rev-Share): it's money that schools earn from their athletic programs which they are now permitted to share directly with the players.

However, not every school is required to participate in Rev-Share. Choosing whether or not to opt in is up to each institution. Some schools with large athletic budgets will share up to the annual revenue-sharing cap -- currently $20.5 million per school for the 2025–26 academic year -- while others may share less or opt out entirely. This seasonal cap is based on a percentage of average revenues from major conferences and will increase as revenues grow over the next decade. The stipulated settlement in *House v. NCAA* ("House Settlement") now allows each Power 4 school to pay a total of $20.5 million to their athletes. This money is referred to as Rev-Share, for the revenue the universities share with the athletes from various income sources, such as ticket sales, television deals, and other streams of revenue. Universities are free to now enter into Rev-Share agreements with college athletes and pay those athletes directly.

When they enter into those agreements, schools can create duration and stability incentives: the Rev-Share agreements can extend over multiple years and can be contingent upon the athlete remaining enrolled at the institution. There can be escalating clauses where the athlete earns more each year with a contract for two to four years. During that time, the agreement would restrict the athlete from entering the portal.

The Rev-Share deals with the school could also include performance-based incentives tied to athletic and academic achievements. Such clauses would reward commitment and discourage opportunistic transfers that are currently plaguing college sports.

If the portal does remain an option under these contracts, universities could include buyout clauses. That would mean that if college athletes want to transfer, they are obligated to pay the school a predetermined amount or percentage of their initial contract value. That buyout fee is usually higher than the player's market value.

These multi-year deals could provide more stability and financial predictability for the athletes, making it less appealing to transfer for potentially better, but uncertain yearly offers.

What Rev-Share Is (And Isn't)

What it is: A school-funded compensation pool, subject to an annual cap, paid under written contracts for roster participation and program obligations. It can include base pay plus incentives (on-field and academic), with clear schedules and conditions. It's basically a salary cap for colleges.

What it isn't: NIL. Rev-Share is not third-party branding money. It does not require ads, posts, or appearances for outside companies. It's not pay routed through boosters or collectives. It's the school paying you to be part of its athletics program under a regulated cap.

How Schools Will Actually Structure Rev-Share

Expect contracts to cover, at a minimum:

- Term & enrollment status: Start/end dates, how redshirt years count, what happens during medical hardship, and whether a coaching change affects obligations.

- Compensation design: Base amount, timing (monthly/quarterly), and escalators for staying multiple years (your language on escalating clauses fits right here).

- Incentives: Performance bonuses (games, awards, starts), academic incentives (GPA/credit thresholds), and compliance bonuses (team/community obligations).

- Portal/transfer mechanics: Your note on restrictions and buyouts is key. If transfer remains an option, expect defined buyout math, notice periods, and repayment triggers spelled out line-by-line.

- Termination & suspension: Grounds (ineligibility, serious misconduct, extended unavailability), cure periods, and partial-pay rules if you're inactive but still enrolled and in good standing.

- Dispute resolution: Investigation process, appeal rights, and whether disputes go to arbitration before any court step.

How Rev-Share Interacts With NIL

Rev-Share doesn't kill NIL -- it separates it. Your school can pay you under Rev-Share and you can still do NIL with real businesses, as long as the NIL deal has a legitimate business purpose, is filed, and doesn't violate team/conflict rules. Think of it as two lanes:

- **Lane 1 (Rev-Share):** School funds. Roster-tied. Salary-style contract. Counts against the school cap.
- **Lane 2 (NIL):** Third-party funds. Promotion/licensing. Deliverables and fair-market value. Reviewed and disclosed.

Key Terms To Look For In Every Rev-Share Deal

Revenue-sharing (Rev-Share) agreements mark a new and significant chapter in college athletics, fundamentally changing how schools compensate players. Unlike traditional NIL deals, Rev-Share contracts are formal agreements directly between the athlete and their university. These contracts tend to resemble professional sports contracts, with a clear

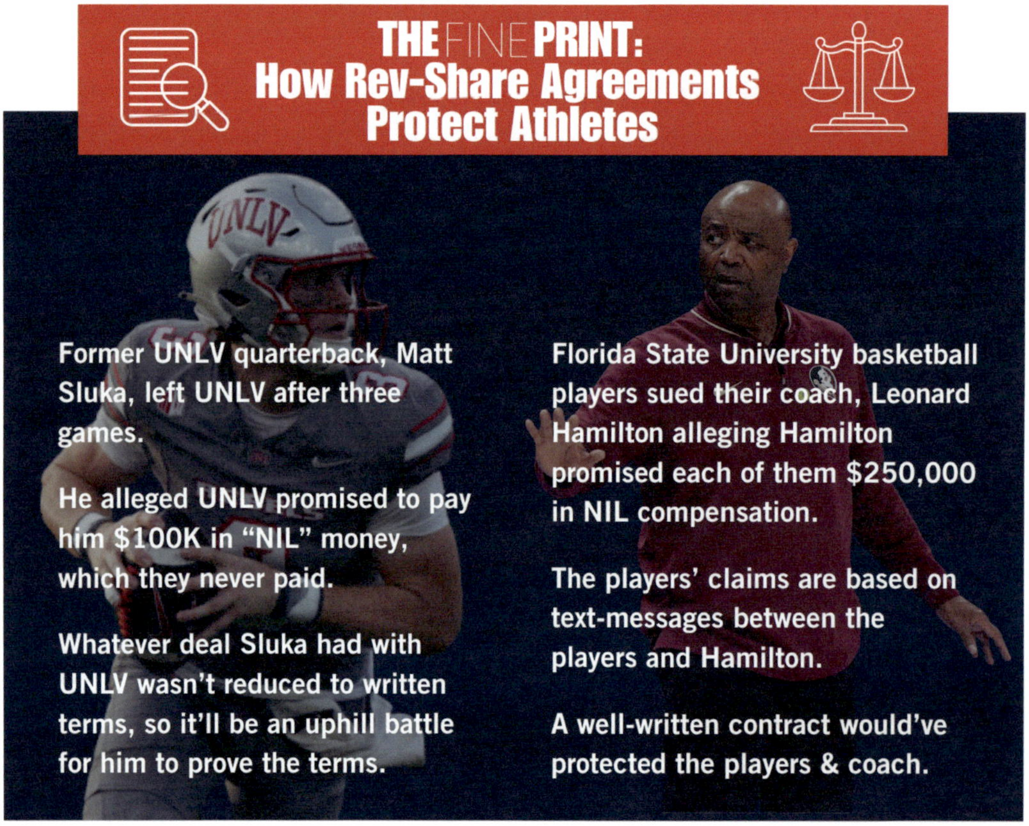

structure, payment schedules, and performance obligations. While NIL deals cannot be linked to you playing sports at a particular school, Rev-Share agreements do exactly that: you are paid by the school to play for that school.

The lawsuits by Sluka and the Florida State basketball players are just the beginning of NIL and Rev-Share legal fights to come.

Former University of Florida quarterback signee Jaden Rashada sued Gators coach Billy Napier last year over an unpaid $13 million NIL deal. And several University of Tulsa players claim they were never paid thousands in NIL commitments made by former coach Kevin Wilson. Entering into contracts for NIL payments or Rev-Share money would protect the athletes, as well as the universities, from potential lawsuits.

Under-the-table incentives or benefits have been happening in college sports for a long time; that's what may have drawn a particular player to a school. For most others, it was a life-long goal to play for their dream school. That's mostly over. Now, it's about getting paid. But now that paying players is legal and out in the open, it's time to bring structure to it. School spirit isn't keeping a player at a particular school anymore, but the right contract will. On the flip side, schools used to use the portal to discard and replace players, but with the right Rev-Share agreement, college athletes can better protect themselves.

That's why understanding the key terms in your Rev-Share agreement is crucial. These terms define your rights, responsibilities, and what you can expect in return for your participation with the school's athletic program.

1. Contract Duration and Term

Rev-Share agreements specify the length of the contract, often covering multiple seasons or academic years. For example, a contract might guarantee payment over a four-year period, aligning with eligibility or scholarship timelines. The term clause may also outline renewal options or conditions for early termination by either party. The term clause should include specific language related to redshirt years.

Example Clause:

"This agreement shall be effective for a term of four (4) years beginning August 1, 2026, and ending July 31, 2030, subject to early termination provisions outlined herein. Any year the player is not on the active roster ("redshirt year") does not count towards the term of this agreement."

2. Salary and Compensation Structure

Similar to professional contracts, Rev-Share deals include a clearly defined salary or payment schedule. Payments might be distributed annually, quarterly, or monthly and may include base salary plus performance-based incentives.

Just as in the "Term" section of the agreement, you should address the compensation structure for any redshirt year.

Example Clause:

"Athlete shall receive an annual salary of $150,000, payable in equal monthly installments, as well as performance bonuses as specified in section 3. Athlete shall receive a reduced salary of $30,000, pro-rated, for any time spent on "redshirt" status."

3. Performance Incentives and Bonuses

Rev-Share contracts can be creatively crafted to include bonuses tied to athletic or academic achievements, such as starting a certain number of games, earning conference awards, individual achievements within your sports, or maintaining minimum GPA levels.

Example Clause:

"Athlete shall receive a $10,000 bonus for each All-Conference selection, $1,000 per home run hit, and a $5,000 bonus for maintaining a GPA above 3.5 per semester."

4. Practice, Competition, and Participation Obligations

The Rev-Share contract will usually detail expectations for attendance at practices, games, promotional events, and other team activities. It clarifies your duties beyond merely showing up on game day, and can have penalties for being late, skipping workouts, and anything else the school is able to bargain for.

Example Clause:

"Athlete agrees to attend all scheduled practices, team meetings, and community events unless excused by the coaching staff."

5. Conduct and Compliance Clauses

These provisions set standards for personal conduct, adherence to NCAA rules, school policies, and expectations regarding public behavior. Violations may trigger penalties, including fines or contract termination.

Example Clause:

"Athlete shall comply with all institutional, NCAA, and team rules. Violations of conduct codes may result in suspension of payments or contract termination."

6. Termination and Buyout Provisions

Rev-Share contracts outline how either party may terminate the agreement, including causes such as injury, academic ineligibility, or breach of contract, and detail financial terms if a buyout applies.

A buyout clause is a contract term that allows one party to end the agreement by paying a predetermined dollar amount to the other party.

Example Clause:

"The University may terminate this agreement upon serious injury preventing participation, academic ineligibility, or violation of conduct rules. Upon termination, the athlete may be entitled to a proportional buyout payment as defined."

THE FINE PRINT: Virginia Tech vs. Redshirt Status

WHO: Virginia Tech football player (name withheld).

WHAT: Player signed a Rev-Share agreement. After requesting to redshirt, the school removed him from the team, cut off payments, and accused him of "fraud."

WHAT WENT WRONG: The Rev-Share agreement allegedly didn't include any clause allowing payment to be stopped for redshirting. The player also hadn't entered the transfer portal, which is a common trigger in other contracts. The player simply mentioning that he is considering redshirting due to a head coaching change triggered the university's actions.

ISSUES: The contract created a blurred line between eligibility decisions and contract rights.

LIKELY RESULT: If the contract has no redshirt clause and payments were guaranteed, the school may have breached the deal.

TAKEAWAY: Revenue share contracts are new and risky. Get legal help before signing. Without protections, schools may interpret the terms however they want, and cut you off without warning.

7. <u>Rights to Name, Image, and Likeness</u>

Even though Rev-Share deals are direct payments from the school, contracts often clarify how NIL rights are handled separately or in conjunction, to avoid conflicts. While universities are not allowed to guarantee an athlete will receive NIL deals if they enroll in the school, the university can help the athlete find NIL deals once the athlete is enrolled.

Example Clause:

"This agreement does not restrict the athlete from entering into NIL agreements with third parties, provided such agreements comply with NCAA and institutional policies. The University will assist the athlete with obtaining NIL deals once the athlete is enrolled at the University."

8. <u>Health, Insurance, and Disability Coverage</u>

Contracts may address medical insurance responsibilities, coverage during athletic participation, and disability protections.

Example Clause:

"The University shall provide medical insurance coverage for injuries sustained during official team activities. In case of permanent disability, the athlete may be eligible for specified compensation under this agreement."

9. <u>Governing Law and Dispute Resolution</u>

This clause specifies which state or jurisdiction's laws govern the agreement and the processes for handling disputes, typically favoring arbitration or mediation before litigation.

Binding arbitration or mediation may be a preferred method to resolve contract disputes because of the finality of the decision and less burdensome process as compared to in-court litigation.

Example Clause:

"This agreement shall be governed by the laws of the State of California. Any disputes arising hereunder shall be resolved through binding arbitration."

Why These Terms Matter

Rev-Share agreements formalize your relationship with the university as more than just an athlete; you become a contracted participant with rights and responsibilities similar to professional players. Knowing these key terms prepares you to negotiate, review, and fulfill your contract with confidence, ensuring you are protected and fully understand your commitments.

Always seek legal and financial advice before signing any Rev-Share contract to make sure your interests are well represented and aligned with your long-term goals. Having a rock-solid Rev-Share agreement will allow you to focus less on the legality of your sport and more on refining your craft to pursue a professional career.

By grasping these contract fundamentals, you take an important step toward empowering yourself in this new era of college athletics.

Differences Between NIL & Rev-Share

Understanding this distinction is crucial. When you hear about large paydays in the media, those seven-figure sums have typically reflected NIL deals funded by collectives -- not university payrolls. Going forward, the rise of revenue sharing means universities will operate a transparent, regulated system to pay athletes directly (Rev-Share), with contracts that look and feel much like pro sports deals, including salary schedules, incentive clauses, and standards of conduct. In a balanced college sports world, Rev-Share is expected to become the primary channel for player compensation, making NIL deals more focused on true endorsements and brand-building rather than recruitment incentives.

NIL VS. REV-SHARE

THIRD-PARTY BUSINESSES	WHO PAYS?	SCHOOL
External funds outside of school's budget	SOURCE OF $	School-generated revenue from defined revenue streams
Payments to promote a product or service	PURPOSE	Compensation to play for a particular school
Does not bind the player to a school for pay	RELATIONSHIP	Player is contractually obligated to play for a school
Marketing agreements tied to personal brand use	NATURE	Professional-style contracts paying salaries over time

HOPKINS LAW
EDUCATED & EMPOWERED ATHLETES

Here are the differences between NIL and Rev-Share deals:

1) Who Pays You

NIL: A third party pays you (brand, business, media company, or collective acting like a broker). The money must be tied to a valid business purpose: promotion, endorsement, appearances, content, or licensing.

Rev-Share: The school pays you directly from defined athletic revenues under a cap (e.g., ~$20.5M per year per Power-4 school at launch). This is roster-tied compensation, managed like a payroll.

2) What Triggers Payment

NIL: Deliverables trigger payment, e.g., social media posts, appearances, ad shoots, or a license for your image. No deliverables = not a compliant NIL deal.

Rev-Share: Participation with the program triggers payment -- being on roster, meeting contract terms, eligibility standards, and program obligations. Deliverables here are team-related, not advertising a product or service.

3) Legal Structure & Core Rules

NIL: Must show a legitimate business purpose and fair-market value (FMV). No pay-for-play, and no clause making pay contingent on enrollment or staying at a specific school. Deals are reviewed, cleared, and disclosed.

Rev-Share: Governed by the House Settlement framework and school policies, overseen by a commission (CSC). Subject to a school-level cap, reporting, and contract standards (term, redshirt treatment, incentives, dispute process).

4) Contract Anatomy

NIL Agreements: Short to mid-length marketing contracts. Define deliverables, timeline, usage rights, approvals, IP/licensing of your NIL, compensation schedule, and termination terms. No enrollment/playing-time contingencies. The NIL agreement cannot extend beyond your college eligibility.

Rev-Share Agreements: Salary-style contracts with base pay, escalators for multi-year stability, performance and academic incentives, portal/transfer terms (including possible buyouts), redshirt/medical language, and conduct provisions.

5) Oversight & Compliance

NIL: Submitted to the designated clearinghouse for review (e.g., Deloitte) and disclosed to your school. The review looks for real deliverables, FMV, and business purposes.

Rev-Share: Monitored by a new enforcement/oversight body, College Sports Commission. The school must track the cap, follow reporting rules, and ensure contracts meet required standards. Disputes can go to arbitration and, if needed, court review.

6) Use of School Marks

NIL: Your NIL is yours, but school logos/marks are separate. To film in official gear or use school trademarks, the brand typically needs a license from the university.

Rev-Share: School branding is generally embedded in team activities, but IP usage for outside commercial work still requires separate permissions.

7) Taxes & Money Management

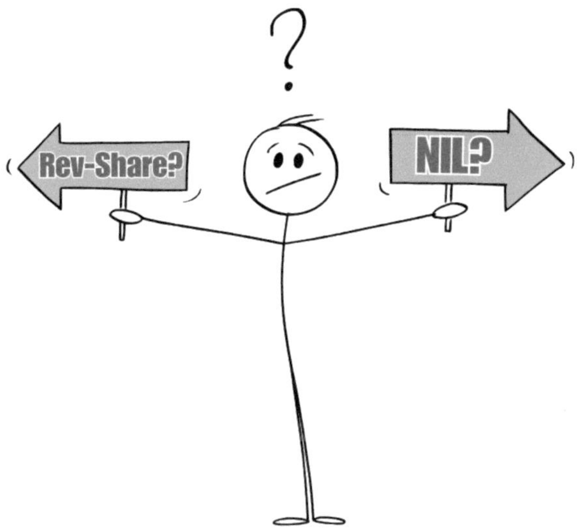

Both are taxable income.

NIL: Often paid to you or your business entity; you'll handle invoicing, 1099-K/1099-NEC, and self-employment tax issues.

Rev-Share: School-paid comp typically arrives on a fixed schedule; plan for withholdings and annual tax reporting.

In either lane, separate your finances, track everything, and set aside money for taxes.

8) Risk Profile

NIL Risks: Non-compliant "pay-for-play" language, no deliverables, overbroad perpetual rights to your NIL, missing disclosures/filings, and rates far above FMV with no proof.

Rev-Share Risks: Ambiguous redshirt treatment, unclear injury/suspension pay rules, buyout math that's harsh or vague, and weak dispute procedures.

9) How They Work Together

Two lanes -- not either/or. You can have a Rev-Share contract with the school and NIL deals with brands. The lanes solve different problems: Rev-Share is transparent, roster-tied compensation; NIL is true marketing/branding income.

As Rev-Share matures, expect NIL to shift back toward authentic endorsements and licensing, with less pressure to function as shadow payroll.

10) Quick Pass/Fail Examples

Compliant NIL: 3 posts + 1 appearance for a local gym that sells to the public; $2,500 at FMV; clear timeline; filed and disclosed; no enrollment clause.

Non-Compliant NIL: $50,000 from a collective "if you enroll and stay," no deliverables, no business purpose.

Clean Rev-Share: 2-year term, base pay with year-2 escalator, defined academic bonuses, redshirt pays 60% base, buyout equals 25% of remaining base, clear dispute process.

Bottom Line

NIL = third-party advertising/licensing money with deliverables, FMV, and disclosures.

Rev-Share = school-paid compensation under a cap, by contract, with incentives and standards.

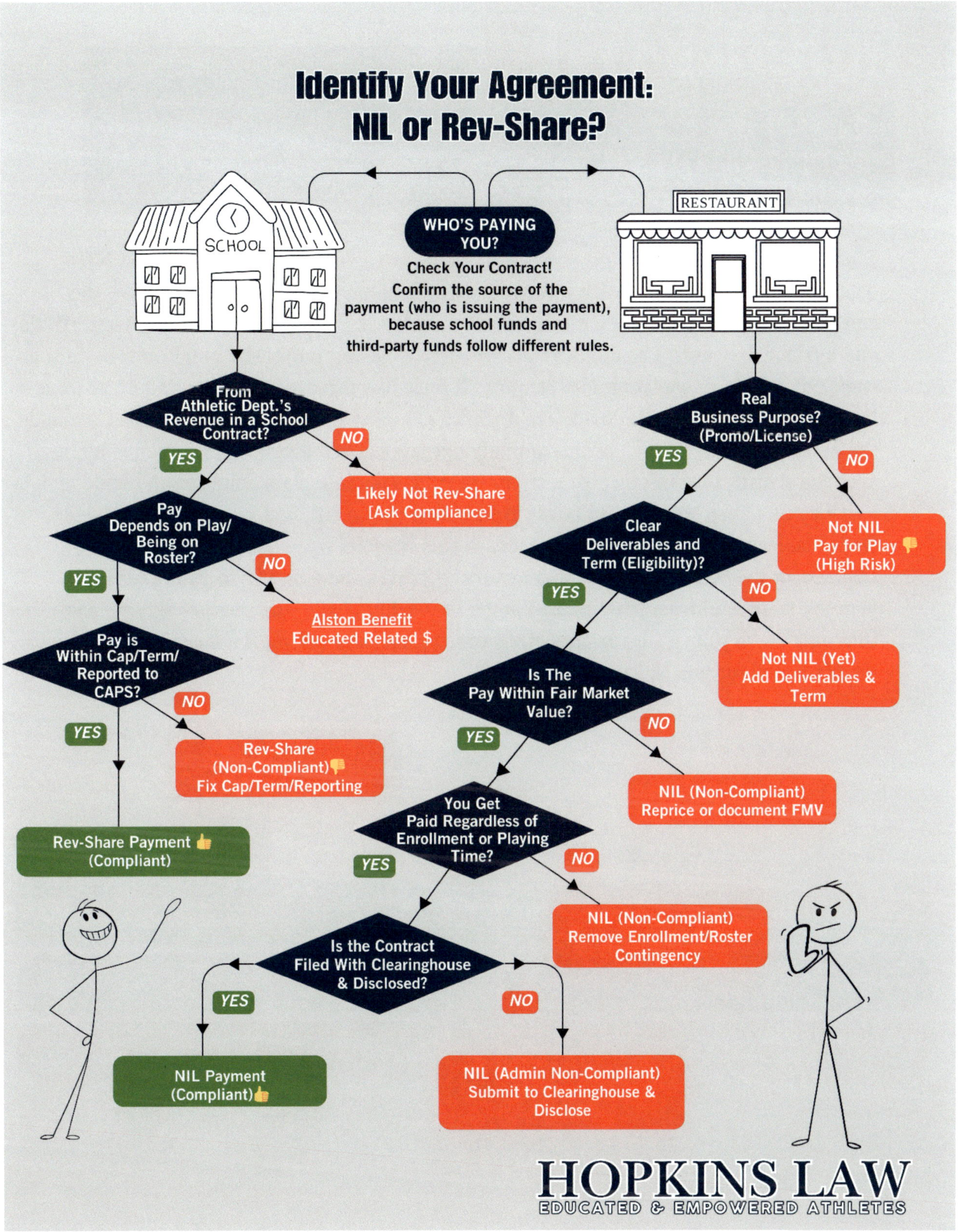
Identify Your Agreement:
NIL or Rev-Share?
WHO'S PAYING YOU?
Check Your Contract!
Confirm the source of the payment (who is issuing the payment), because school funds and third-party funds follow different rules.
SCHOOL
RESTAURANT
From Athletic Dept.'s Revenue in a School Contract?
YES
NO
Likely Not Rev-Share [Ask Compliance]
Pay Depends on Play/ Being on Roster?
YES
NO
Alston Benefit
Educated Related $
Pay is Within Cap/Term/ Reported to CAPS?
YES
NO
Rev-Share (Non-Compliant) Fix Cap/Term/Reporting
Rev-Share Payment (Compliant)
Real Business Purpose? (Promo/License)
YES
NO
Not NIL Pay for Play (High Risk)
Clear Deliverables and Term (Eligibility)?
YES
NO
Not NIL (Yet) Add Deliverables & Term
Is The Pay Within Fair Market Value?
YES
NO
NIL (Non-Compliant) Reprice or document FMV
You Get Paid Regardless of Enrollment or Playing Time?
YES
NO
NIL (Non-Compliant) Remove Enrollment/Roster Contingency
Is the Contract Filed With Clearinghouse & Disclosed?
YES
NO
NIL Payment (Compliant)
NIL (Admin Non-Compliant) Submit to Clearinghouse & Disclose
HOPKINS LAW
EDUCATED & EMPOWERED ATHLETES

MODULE FIVE

CONTRACTS, COMPLIANCE & FUTURE RISKS IN NIL & REV-SHARE

Picture this: your phone dings; your agent texts you a "final draft" of the Pepsi NIL contract, your inbox pings with a Rev-Share addendum from the university GM, the compliance department wants disclosures by Friday, a CPA asks for last quarter's 1099s, and a friend forwards a headline about athletes becoming university employees -- right as a rumor of a Title IX violation hits campus. It feels like three systems booting up at once -- legal, financial, and reputational -- and you're expected to run them all. Module Five pulls the curtain back on how all of this actually operates. We'll dissect contracts line by line, spot the clauses that can trap you, translate rulebooks into plain English, and build simple routines that keep your pay on track, your status compliant, and your future protected. Once you learn and practice the concepts in this Module, responding to the litany of requests at the beginning of this paragraph will feel second nature to you. You'll feel yourself transcend from reacting to things, to moving pieces like chess -- signing contracts that only serve your goals, documenting your moves, and asking the questions that expose what's useful for you and your business.

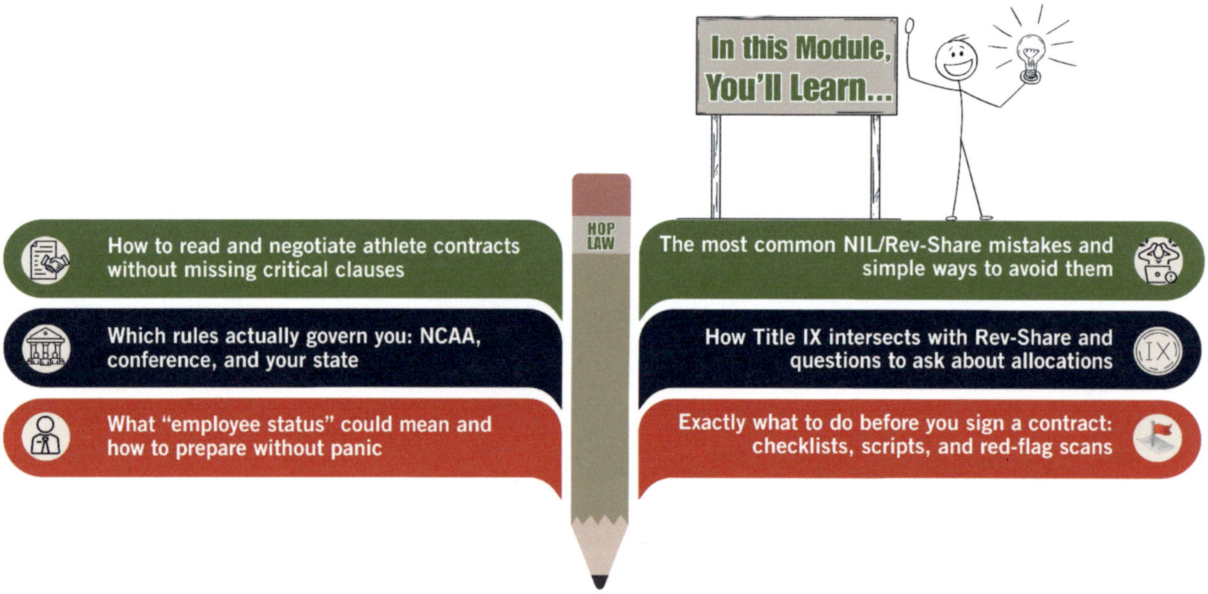

Contracts 101: What To Know Before You Sign

Entering into contracts is a major step in your journey as a college athlete involved in NIL (Name, Image, Likeness) and Rev-Share deals. Contracts are legally binding agreements that define your rights, obligations, and protections. Understanding what you're agreeing to before signing is crucial for safeguarding your finances, eligibility, and personal brand. This section provides a thorough overview of key contract fundamentals every athlete should know.

What Is a Contract?

A contract is a written or verbal agreement between parties that creates mutual obligations enforceable by law. In NIL and Rev-Share deals, contracts specify details like payment, usage rights of your NIL, deliverables, timelines, and termination conditions.

Important Contract Terms to Understand

Compensation: How much you'll be paid and payment schedule. Watch for unclear or performance-based conditions.

Length and Termination: Duration of the contract ("term") and how either party can end the agreement.

Rights Granted: What rights you give the company to use your NIL -- scope, territory, and duration. Avoid overly broad or perpetual rights.

Obligations/Deliverables: What you must do (e.g., appearances, social media posts) and consequences of failing to perform.

Exclusivity: Whether you're restricted from doing similar deals with competitors.

Non-Compete/Non-Disparagement: Clauses that limit your ability to work with others or speak negatively about the entity on the other side of the contract.

Indemnification/Hold-Harmless: Who takes responsibility if legal issues arise related to the contract.

Governing Law and Dispute Resolution: Which state's laws apply and how disputes will be resolved (mediation, arbitration, court).

Why Reading Every Clause Matters

Contracts can contain complex legal language that affects your rights and future opportunities. Missing unfavorable terms can lead to loss of control over your NIL, financial penalties, or eligibility risks. Taking time to understand every section allows you to negotiate better terms or reject harmful clauses.

Red Flags to Watch For

- Unclear payment terms or delayed payment schedules.
- Unlimited or very broad use of your NIL beyond the deal's life.
- Excessive obligations without clear compensation.
- Automatic renewals without notice.
- Waivers of your rights to challenge the agreement.
- Lack of compliance assurances with NCAA or university rules.

The Role of Legal and Compliance Professionals

Consulting with a qualified attorney and your school's compliance office before signing contracts is critical. Experts can:

- Explain legal jargon in plain language.
- Ensure deals align with school, conference, NCAA, and state rules.
- Negotiate terms that protect your interests.
- Spot hidden risks or requirements.

Practical Tips Before Signing

- Never sign contracts on the spot. Take time to review.
- Ask for all contract terms in writing.

- ❖ Keep copies of every agreement and correspondence.
- ❖ Understand tax implications of payments.
- ❖ Make sure contract timelines fit your schedule and priorities.
- ❖ Clarify any ambiguous terms before agreeing.

Contracts are the foundation of your business relationships and financial future as an athlete. Armed with knowledge and professional guidance, you can confidently navigate agreements, protect your brand, and maximize your opportunities without sacrificing control or security.

Common Mistakes To Avoid When Signing Deals

Entering into NIL and Rev-Share agreements is an exciting milestone in any college athlete's journey, but it comes with significant responsibility. Many athletes face pitfalls that can jeopardize their financial security, eligibility, and reputation. It's important to understand the common mistakes outlined below before signing any deal. Having a solid understanding of this info will help you protect yourself and maximize your opportunities.

1. Signing Contracts Without Fully Understanding Terms

One of the biggest mistakes athletes make is blindly signing contracts without carefully reading and understanding every clause. Many NIL deals come from small businesses or individuals without formal legal support, which can lead to ambiguous or unfavorable language, such as vague compensation terms, excessive obligations, or overly broad rights to your NIL.

Avoid This By: Consulting a lawyer or compliance officer before committing. Don't let excitement cloud your judgment -- clarity now prevents costly regrets later.

2. Ignoring NCAA, Conference, or State Rules

Failing to comply with the ever-evolving rules governing NIL and Rev-Share can lead to penalties or loss of eligibility. Each university and conference may have specific policies on reporting, permissible activities, and third-party relationships. Additionally, your state's NIL laws add another layer of regulation.

Avoid This By: Working closely with your school's compliance office and regularly reviewing updates. Make sure every deal is properly disclosed and structured to stay within the rules.

3. Treating NIL Earnings Like Free Money

Landing your first NIL or Rev-Share payment can feel life-changing, but many athletes overspend quickly or don't budget for future needs. This change in lifestyle can lead to financial instability once contracts end or income fluctuates.

Avoid This By: Creating and sticking to a budget, tracking all income and expenses, and prioritizing saving and investing early. Treat each paycheck as an opportunity to build long-term wealth, not just immediate gratification.

4. Not Paying Taxes or Mismanaging Tax Obligations

All NIL and Rev-Share income is taxable, and unlike salaries from typical jobs, taxes are not automatically withheld. Missing tax payments or misunderstanding your obligations can cause significant financial problems down the road.

Avoid This By: Setting aside part of every payment for taxes and consulting a tax professional familiar with athlete finances. Stay on top of deadlines for estimated taxes and reporting income properly.

5. Giving Up Too Much Control Over Your Brand

Some athletes unknowingly sign contracts that give companies excessive rights to their name, image, and likeness -- sometimes for the entire college career or beyond. This lack of control can limit your future opportunities and leave you without compensation for deals others make using your brand.

Avoid This By: Making sure contracts limit use of your NIL to specific terms (time frame, media types, geography) and preserve your right to negotiate future deals.

6. Overcommitting and Losing Focus on Academics and Athletics

Balancing multiple NIL deals alongside the demands of being a student-athlete is challenging. Taking on too many commitments or deals that interfere with training, competitions, or studies can harm both your athletic career and academic progress.

Avoid This By: Setting priorities, managing time wisely, and choosing deals that fit your schedule without detracting from your main responsibilities.

7. Missing Opportunities with Local Businesses

Many athletes overlook simpler, local sponsorship opportunities because they target only large national brands or high-profile endorsements. Local businesses often represent attainable, mutually beneficial partnerships.

Avoid This By: Proactively reaching out to community businesses you support. Build partnerships that boost local economies and your brand with less competition for attention.

8. Failing to Use Professional Representation

Attempting to handle negotiations alone without professional advice increases the risk of unfavorable deals or legal issues.

Avoid This By: Seeking attorneys, agents, or advisors experienced in NIL and Rev-Share contracts. They can protect your interests, optimize deal terms, and ensure compliance.

Avoiding these common mistakes requires discipline, education, and a strong team around you that you can trust. With the right approach, you can turn NIL and Rev-Share opportunities into lasting assets for your future, both on and off the field.

This book, your school's resources, and trusted legal and financial professionals are critical allies to guide you in making smart, empowered decisions throughout your career.

Rules & Regulations: NCAA, Conference, and State Laws

As college athletes step into the new era of NIL and revenue sharing opportunities, it's essential to understand the complex web of rules and regulations that govern how you can be paid. These rules come from the NCAA, your athletic conference, and the laws passed by individual states. Knowing how each of these layers work together (and sometimes conflict) is critical to protecting your eligibility and maximizing your opportunities.

NCAA Rules and Recent Changes

The NCAA has dramatically shifted its policies since 2021 to allow athletes to monetize their name, image, and likeness. The association now requires all NIL deals to be reported and ensures transparency in how payments are made. Under the most recent rules aligned with the House Settlement, schools are prohibited from guaranteeing third-party NIL contracts or payments to athletes. This means your university can't promise a booster or collective will pay you; it must be a valid business deal directly between you and the third party. Schools can, however, broker those deals. They just can't make any guarantee that a deal will happen just because you enroll in their particular school.

The NCAA also demands that any NIL agreement with third parties must have a valid business purpose related to genuine marketing or promotions of products and services. Deals that look like pay-for-play without actual marketing or promotional work may be scrutinized or rejected.

The NCAA has also started allowing schools to enter direct revenue-sharing agreements with athletes. These agreements allow schools to directly pay players from certain revenue streams -- though participation is optional and not all schools have opted in. New Division I rules require comprehensive reporting of NIL and Rev-Share agreements to maintain accountability and compliance.

Conference Policies

Your athletic conference may have additional rules that complement or enhance NCAA regulations. Some Power Four conferences, for example, have implemented stricter guidelines on NIL disclosures, representation, and financial literacy education for athletes. Conferences often coordinate with universities to ensure fair play and compliance within their member schools. It's vital to check your conference's specific approach because these policies impact what kind of deals you can do and how you report them.

State Laws and Legislation

More than 30 states plus the District of Columbia have passed their own NIL laws (with more states pending NIL legislation), creating a patchwork of rules that can vary widely depending on where your school is located. Typically, if your school is in a state with NIL legislation, you must comply with both NCAA and state laws. If there is no state law, institutional and conference policies usually govern.

California was the first state to enact NIL legislation in 2019. Under California law, schools are not allowed to prohibit athletes from pursuing NIL opportunities. The California law also requires transparency in these deals and provides certain protections for athletes, including privacy provisions and restrictions on how NIL income is taxed or reported. California's approach has influenced other states and pushed for more athlete-friendly policies nationwide.

Florida's NIL law, one of the most comprehensive, mandates that universities provide educational resources about NIL, requires disclosure of any agreements involving athletes, and prohibits schools from interfering in or restricting NIL activities. Florida has also embraced revenue sharing options, allowing schools to share a percentage of certain athletic revenues with players if they choose.

Federal Legislation

On the federal legislation side, two major House bills have been floated as possible solutions: the SCORE Act and the CARA bill. The SCORE Act (H.R. 4312) proposed a national NIL system and is written broadly enough to touch both NIL and compensation "related to participation" on a college team (which is where the Rev-Share conversation lives). It also takes a strong position on federal preemption (federal rules overriding many state laws) and includes language about student-athletes not being treated as employees of schools/conferences/associations, plus other structural provisions meant to stabilize the competitive landscape. The SCORE Act is not likely to be passed as it appears to have been abandoned.

The College Athletics Reform Act (CARA) (H.R. 6350) moves in a different direction by setting up a bipartisan commission structure and also explicitly anchors "athlete agent" to the definition in SPARTA. CARA basically signals that agent regulation is part of the federal conversation, not an afterthought.

Beyond those, there are other federal proposals floating that matter because they show where lawmakers' heads are at: for example, the Student Athlete Fairness and Enforcement (SAFE) Act (S. 2932) is a wide-scope Senate proposal that bundles NIL rights and athlete protections with items that spill into the college sports revenue ecosystem, with proposals such as an athlete ombuds office and even broadcast/media rights components.

And there are additional House efforts pitched as "national standards" bills (one example is the College SPORTS Act, introduced in mid-2025), which reinforces the point that Congress is still shopping for a federal framework -- even while the post-House settlement college world is trying to implement the new NIL and Rev-Share rules through sport-industry mechanisms like the College Sports Commission.

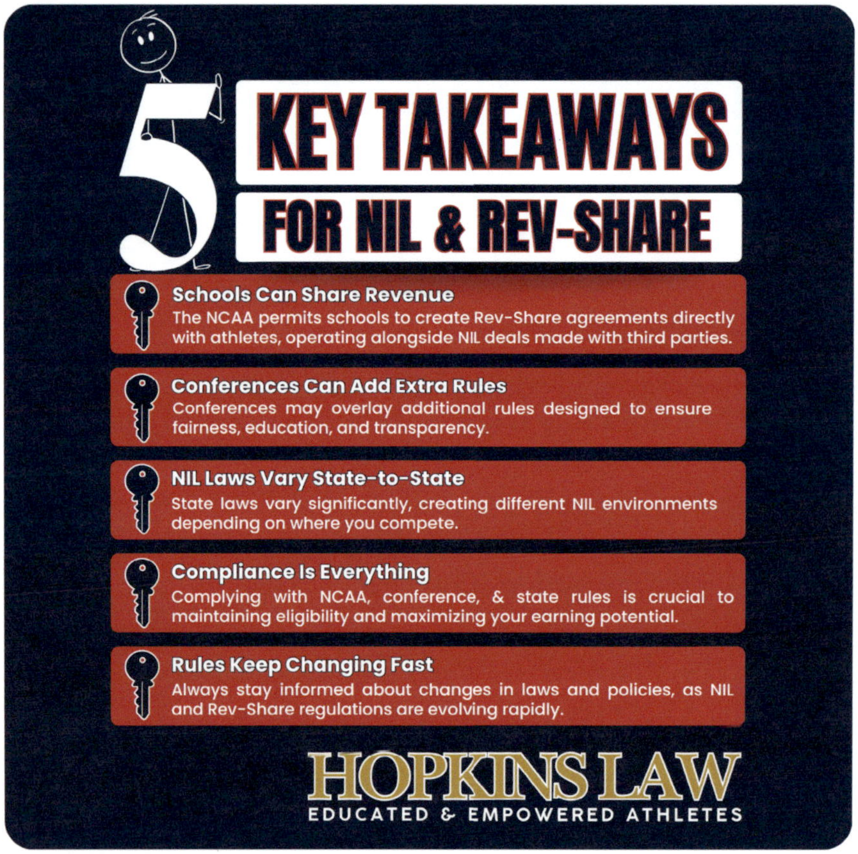

This layered regulatory environment means your best defense is knowledge and proactive compliance. Use this book/workshop, your school's compliance office, and available legal and financial advisers to ensure your deals are above board, protective of your interests, and aligned with the governing rules of your sport.

How Rev-Share Distribution Will Impact Title IX

Sports programs at NCAA Power 4 schools generated almost $6 billion ($5,772,515,049) combined. Women's sports accounted for approximately 2.2% of that figure, while men's sports generated approximately 97.8%. In dollars, women generated $128,415,761 and men brought in $5,644,099,288. These figures represent the revenue generated by the universities, not money from athletes' NIL deals.

Current NIL deals are paid by third parties, not the universities. The *House v. NCAA* Stipulated Settlement ("House Settlement") allows each Power 4 school to pay a total of $20.5 million directly to their student-athletes (Rev-Share). Each school will create their own pay structure for their athletes. Inevitably, some athletes will be paid more than others. The question is, if male athletes are paid disproportionately more of that money than female athletes, is that a violation of Title IX?

What is Title IX?

Title IX is a federal civil rights law that requires that male and female student-athletes to receive equitable treatment and benefits in federally funded education programs, which includes athletics.

That sounds vague. What the law really requires is equality in three areas: 1) effective accommodation of student interests and abilities (known as participation); 2) athletic financial assistance (scholarships); and 3) what's known as the "Laundry List," which is 11 categories of benefits, including equipment and supplies, scheduling of games and practice times, travel and daily per diem allowances, access to tutoring, coaching, locker rooms, practice and competitive facilities, medical and training facilities and services, publicity, recruitment of student athletes and support services.

BROWN UNIVERSITY: A TITLE IX CAUTIONARY CASE FOR COLLEGE GMS

COHEN V. BROWN UNIVERSITY 879 F. SUPP. 185 (1ST CIRCUIT)

- A class-action Title IX case brought by female college athletes when Brown reduced the volleyball and gymnastics teams from fully-funded varsity programs to club teams.
- Brown argued no Title IX violation occurred because they also reduced two male varisty sports.

THE COURT RULED:

- PARTICIPATION GAP: Women are 51.14% of students but only 38.13% of athletes (13.01% shortfall).
- SLOTS SKEWED MALE: 555 men's vs. 342 women's opportunities (incl. donor-funded: 76 men, 30 women).
- NO ONGOING EXPANSION SHOWN: Since 1977 Brown added only two women's teams (indoor track '82, skiing '94); cutting men's teams doesn't count as expansion.
- Brown's actions violated Title IX's Equal Opportunity requirement.
- EO in this case involved Brown not providing a selection of sports and levels of competition to effectively accommodate the interests and abilities of the women at Brown.

TITLE IX REQUIRES:

- PRONG 1: Substantial proportionality: Each sex's share of varsity participation ≈ its share of undergraduate enrollment.
- PRONG 2: Continuing expansion of opportunities for the underrepresented sex.
- PRONG 3: Full and effective accommodation of the underrepresented sex's interests/abilities(e.g., elevating/adding teams when there's unmet demand).
- ALSO: There's a separate athletic financial-aid proportionality requirement (fair scholarship dollars).

WHY IT MATTERS:

- ATHLETICALLY RELATED FINANCIAL AID MUST BE AWARDED TO MEN AND WOMEN IN PROPORTION TO THEIR PARTICIPATION WITH NO "REVENUE SPORT" EXCUSE FOR SKEWED AID. IF REV-SHARE IS DEEMED AID, THEN INEQUITABLE DISPERSEMENT COULD BE A TITLE IX VIOLATION.

Compliance with Title IX is evaluated globally at a university, across entire athletic programs rather than individual sports. Doing so allows for differences in the type and number of opportunities offered to each sex, provided the opportunities meet the interests and needs of underrepresented groups. Title IX also prohibits economic justifications for discrimination, meaning schools cannot prioritize revenue-generating sports like football at the expense of equitable opportunities for women.

Who Should Get What in the House Settlement?

Despite Title IX protections, demand for the largest share of the $20.5 million will be from the highest generating sports at any particular university. Statistically, that sport will be a men's sport, either football or basketball. Those sports account for 77.4% and 18.3% of the total revenue share, respectively.

Such a plan is rooted in economic logic, but not fully aligned with Title IX's principles of equity. If a university's allocation plan for that $20.5 million leaves little money left over for the school to field competitive women's teams or provide comparable scholarships, training, or resources, then that allocation plan violates Title IX.

In practical terms, it's understood that there is already a significant gap between men's and women's sports at colleges. The men's facilities for higher revenue-generating sports are of higher quality than women's facilities, recruitment budgets aren't equitable, men's sports even get the more desirable practice times, all Title IX violations. Those violations, among others, will be exacerbated if the schools' allocation of the $20.5 million increases that gap in participation opportunities between male and female athletes.

Arthur Bryant, an attorney who has represented both female and male athletes in gender equity lawsuits against schools like San Diego State, Clemson, and Oregon, reported, "Most colleges in America are violating Title IX and depriving women of equal opportunities to participate in intercollegiate athletics. The federal government isn't enforcing the law and making them comply like it should. So this illegal sex discrimination is continuing. If girls and women want it to stop, they have to be willing to stand up, fight, and sue."

What's Likely to be Done?

Undoubtedly, the schools will end up paying a small handful of players -- football and basketball players -- large paychecks. All other athletes, from both the women's and men's sports, such as softball, baseball, track and field, will earn substantially lower salaries. Even male athletes on football and basketball teams will get paid either low or no money from the revenue-sharing monies. Disproportionately, however, women's sports will receive less revenue-sharing money.

Even if schools violate Title IX under the new revenue-sharing rules, shamefully, nothing will be done to enforce the lack of compliance. A report publicly released by the U.S. Government Accountability Office confirmed what university officials and athletes already know: Title IX is routinely violated and rarely enforced.

The GAO report, aptly titled "Education Should Improve its Title IX Enforcement Efforts," found that during the 2021-22 academic year, 93% of universities had female athletic participation rates lower than their enrollment rate, while 63% of schools had participation-enrollment gaps of 10% or more. Overall, the athletic participation rate for collegiate women was 14% less than their enrollment rate.

To date, no school has ever had their funding pulled because of Title IX noncompliance, nor been sued by the federal government. With the new rules allowing universities to pay college athletes, Title IX violations will get worse, absent some form of oversight and enforcement, but even then history teaches us that nothing is likely to be done about it.

So where does that leave us? Perhaps this may be more educational than step-by-step guidance, but Title IX isn't a vague ideal -- it's enforceable law. It's a legal measuring stick the school has to meet across participation, scholarships, and the "Laundry List." If a Rev-Share plan drains resources or opportunities from women's sports and widens the participation gap, the school is building a compliance problem into its payroll.

If you're facing a Title IX situation, demand answers to the relevant questions. Every university is legally required to have a Title IX Coordinator. Start by posing the following questions to the coordinator: How is the school allocating the $20.5 million and what's their stated rationale? Does that plan keep participation opportunities, scholarship dollars, coaching, facilities, travel, and support services on track for women's teams? What happens to women's recruiting budgets under the university's Rev-Share framework? If the answers are nebulous or "we'll see," that's a red flag.

Finally, remember this is not about pitting athletes against each other. It's about forcing universities to budget in compliance with the law: pay athletes transparently and protect equity. The two can coexist if schools plan for both from day one -- set Rev-Share, preserve scholarships, keep the Laundry List balanced, and publish what they're doing. If they're unwilling or unable to do so, the same courts that opened the door to athlete pay are at the disposal of athletes who feel their rights have been violated.

Will College Athletes Become University Employees?

There's a lawsuit, *Johnson v. NCAA*, making its way through the courts that asks a direct question: are college athletes employees for the time they spend representing their schools? In July, 2024, the Third Circuit determined it's a possibility they could be under the Fair Labor Standards Act (FLSA) and sent the case back to the district court to apply the multi-factor "economic realities" test. That ruling created a circuit split, which means this issue could end up at the U.S. Supreme Court. In the meantime, the district court is working through the factors, the NCAA and co-defendants still have live motions, and, depending on how this plays out, there's a real possibility of substantial back-pay claims by current and former athletes for past seasons.

Running alongside Johnson is the *House v. NCAA* settlement, approved in June 2025. House sets out a framework for direct athlete compensation: beginning July 2025, Division I schools can share a defined slice of athletics revenue with student-athletes under a capped, reported system -- what everyone now calls Rev-Share. *House* is about how schools can pay athletes lawfully within college sports; *Johnson* is about whether athletes are employees under federal labor law. Those are different questions. *House* answers the "how" for student status; *Johnson* tests the "who" under employment law, with broader consequences, especially for back pay.

If a court ultimately classifies athletes as employees, pay doesn't disappear -- it changes legal categories. Under employment law, compensation becomes wages/bonuses set by the school (and potentially by a collective bargaining agreement if athletes unionize), not a built-in right to a share of university revenue. In other words: there is no automatic legal entitlement to Rev-Share just because someone is an employee, any more than an Amazon employee is automatically entitled to revenue. Schools could keep a revenue-pool concept, convert it to wages and bonuses, or shift to straight salaries; the law cares that employees are paid lawfully, not that pay must be a "share."

Employee status would introduce practical obligations. Non-exempt workers must be paid at least minimum wage (and overtime, if applicable). That forces schools to define and track compensable hours -- practice, meetings, travel, media, rehab -- and ensure pay clears legal floors. Some athletes could earn more based on role, time, or negotiated terms; differential pay is lawful so long as it isn't based on sex or other protected characteristics. Benefits aren't automatic under the FLSA; eligibility for health coverage, retirement, and other benefits would depend on plan rules, ACA full-time status, state law (for public schools), and any collective bargaining outcomes. Workers' compensation coverage typically follows from employee status.

Title IX remains in the picture, but its role shifts. Title IX will still govern the overall equity of an athletics program inside a federally funded university, yet employment pay levels are principally analyzed under labor and anti-discrimination laws (FLSA, Title VII, Equal Pay Act). Title IX has never required identical wages across different jobs; it forbids sex-based disparities in program opportunities and benefits. If schools retain a House-style Rev-Share for students, those dollars and access still need to be budgeted with equity in mind. If athletes become employees and schools transition to wages, the equity analysis will run through employment law standards while Title IX continues to police the broader treatment of men's and women's programs.

Here's where wages and rev-share converge. Once athletes become employees, schools will have to pay each athlete at least minimum wage for playing a sport. But some athletes will be paid more than others. Inevitably, the softball player who receives just a few thousand dollars will file suit when their school forks out over $1 million to a football player. Some feel such disparate pay would violate Title IX protections. They argue all athletes should be paid the same, no different than students who work in the bookstore.

The counterpoint is straightforward: employment law allows different pay for different jobs and market values, so long as sex is not the reason for the difference. The argument that all student-athletes should be paid equally is akin to sentiments surrounding unequal pay between WNBA and NBA players. Some feel it is unfair for the lowest paid NBA player -- say, Bronny James at $1,157,153 -- to make almost a million dollars more than star WNBA player Caitlin Clark at her $76,535 salary. The counterargument is that the NBA brought in $11.34 billion last season, while the WNBA generated $200 million, but with expenses, operated in the negative.

The same can be said for non-revenue-generating sports at the university level. Often, the football and basketball programs at Division I schools fund most, if not all, other sports, which consistently operate in a deficit. Overall, there are only a handful of athletic departments in all of college sports that turn a profit. But students at a university are not professional athletes (at least, not yet). Because of that, they are afforded the right under Title IX to be treated equally. Simplistically speaking, Title IX is a federal civil rights law that requires male and female student-athletes to receive equitable treatment and benefits in federally funded education programs, which includes athletics.

If all student athletes were treated equally under the new revenue-sharing model, each of the approximate 480 athletes at a Division I school would receive $48,125 per year, no matter their sex or sport. But if we choose to be more accurate and remove "student" from the student-athlete moniker, which was placed on college athletes in order to prevent paying them in the first place, the path forward becomes more clear. Once athletes become employees, courts will be far less likely to find schools have violated Title IX if they pay male athletes (football and basketball players) more than female athletes. While it's true that Title IX applies to employees of universities (for sex-based discrimination), all pay doesn't need to be equal across the board between men and women employees; schools can pay employees based on the value that particular employee brings to the campus.

In that case, it would be reasonable to pay an individual who is responsible for bringing in millions of dollars to the university a substantially higher salary than the person who generates virtually no revenue. That's the legal landscape: *House* sets a compliant path for direct student compensation starting in July, 2025; *Johnson* could redefine the relationship under the FLSA and invite a wave of back-pay claims. If employee status arrives, money won't vanish. It will be re-labeled, time-tracked, taxed through payroll, and, in many places, bargained. The real question for each school isn't whether to pay; it's which framework they'll use -- and whether they can do it without tripping over the laws that now apply.

Does Private Equity Belong In College Sports? The Fine Print Behind Fast Cash

Here's the setup. The Big Ten Conference -- home to powerhouse schools like Michigan, Ohio State, USC, and Penn State -- is considering selling a 10% ownership stake in a new business unit called Big Ten Enterprises for $2.4 billion. That business unit would hold all of the conference's money-making assets -- media rights, sponsorships, brand licensing, the whole commercial engine. In exchange, the buyer -- a University of California–affiliated pension investment fund (not a private equity firm in name, but institutional capital all the same) -- would receive a minority ownership stake that gives it a share of future profits but no control over operations. The deal would effectively value the Big Ten at around $20 billion and send hundreds of millions to each of its 18 member schools.

While the Big Ten deal may not get finalized, it's the next logical step in the same story -- college sports turning into a financial marketplace where athletic departments behave like media corporations and private investors want in.

If you're wondering why a college sports conference would need outside cash, you already know the answer: the math doesn't add up anymore. Stadium projects cost hundreds of millions. Coaches' contracts have ballooned. The new revenue-sharing payments to athletes (roughly $20 million a year per school) under the House settlement will further burden athletic departments. These departments, even at the top tier schools, are debt-heavy and running razor-thin margins despite record revenues. The Big Ten has a $7 billion media deal that runs through 2030, but a lot of that money is already spent. That's why we're seeing individual teams starting to make their own deals with private equity firms.
Enter the financial "solution." A $2.4 billion cash infusion sounds like a rescue plan. But some university regents have compared it to a payday loan -- trading away long-term equity for a short-term budget patch. The University of Michigan's board blasted the proposal as reckless, calling it "contrived urgency" and questioning why the conference

needs to "sell itself to save college sports." They're not wrong to be skeptical. The deal would extend the Big Ten's grant of media rights through 2046, effectively locking all schools in place and locking potential profits -- good or bad -- for decades.

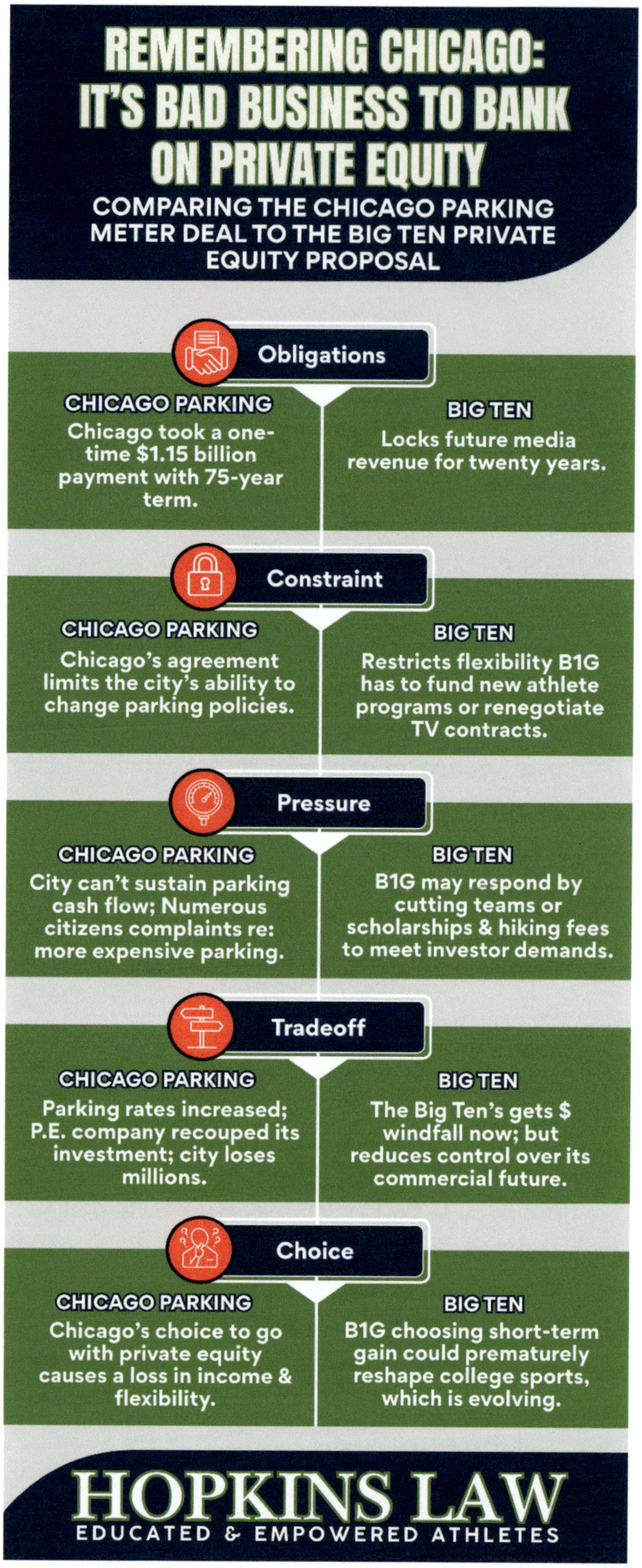

Here's what it looks like in real terms: college sports are now so deeply commercialized that university conferences are creating corporations and selling off pieces of themselves the same way pro leagues sell franchise stakes. For athletes, that's confirmation of something the courts already made clear -- the system isn't amateur. Everyone is monetizing the game. The predictable wave of private capital interest shows that college athletics have reached the asset class stage: a product valuable enough to attract institutional investors looking for returns.

So when athletes see administrators saying "there's no money" for salaries, perks, or post-career benefits, it's worth remembering that the same schools are now literally offering slices of the enterprise to investment funds. They see the future value. They just want to monetize it on their terms before labor costs (that means athlete pay) rise any higher. That's why you will start seeing company patches on jerseys.

If the Big Ten closes this deal, expect it to become a blueprint for other leagues -- SEC, ACC, Big 12 -- all now facing the same rising costs under new revenue-sharing laws. That's how fast the business model of college sports is shifting: from supposedly "amateur" athletics to billion-dollar capitalization events. And if private capital is willing to value a college conference like a pro sports league, it's long past time the athletes themselves are valued -- and compensated -- the same way.

The Big Ten's $2.4 billion private equity deal plan isn't about athletes on its face, but it absolutely involves you. Every dollar of that deal is being justified as a way to sustain the new system of athlete pay. That's what "revenue pressures" means in plain English: the conference knows it has to share money directly with players because of the House settlement, and wants investors to cover the tab. The same goes for individual schools.

When you see these private equity deals being done, understand what that really signals -- college sports are officially trading equity like a company, not just selling sponsorships or TV ads. The upside is that it confirms you're part of an enterprise valuable enough for billion-dollar investors. The risk is that decisions about your sport -- scheduling, media exposure, spending cuts -- may soon be influenced by financial stakeholders who never step on a field. That's why understanding the business side isn't optional anymore.

Solving The Unregulated Agent Problem

Perhaps the most troubling part of the new rules governing NIL and Rev-Share agreements is that there are no real regulations protecting college athletes from people claiming to be agents. Neither the NCAA nor the CSC have requirements for people who represent college athletes as part of their NIL or Rev-Share agreements. Anyone is free to call themselves an "NIL agent," or "college sports agent," and represent any college athlete when it comes to NIL and Rev-Share agreements. There is no mandatory course, no test, and no licensing; all that's needed is a business card and the addition of "NIL agent" in their Instagram bio.

Prior to this new NIL world, a sports agent who wanted to work with college athletes was signing that athlete to an agency contract in order for the athlete to turn professional. Those were agents that were regulated by the NFL or NBA. Now, with the new rules in college/amateur sports, there's been a flock of new "agents" who are representing high school and college athletes for NIL and Rev-Share agreements, not to turn pro. To be clear, NIL and Rev-Share deals involve two different types of representation (or at least they should). One -- NIL -- is supposed to be tied to marketing value (true NIL endorsements, licensing, merch, appearances), while the other -- Rev-Share -- is tied to participation in college sports (salary-like payments in a Rev-Share structure, or NIL arrangements that function as a proxy for salary for being on a roster).

Those two buckets are not the same thing. They should not be valued the same way when it comes to agency contracts. And if we don't draw the line clearly, athletes will keep signing contracts where the "representative" gets paid like a marketer even when the underlying money is essentially compensation for being on the roster.

The Current Legal Landscape: Regulation Exists — But It's Fragmented, Uneven, and Outdated by Design

When I used the words "unregulated agent" above, that's not literally true. There is regulation on paper. But in practice, it's fragmented across federal law, state law, and school policy, and it certainly did not contemplate the current NIL/Rev-Share reality.

Federal law: SPARTA is real -- and the FTC just put it back in play

The somewhat relevant federal statute is the Sports Agent Responsibility and Trust Act ("SPARTA"), codified at 15 U.S.C. §§ 7801–7807. SPARTA is a law that prohibits certain conduct by sports agents relating to contracts with student-athletes, including recruiting through false or misleading statements or providing "anything of value" before an agency contract is signed.

SPARTA matters even more today because the FTC has now signaled that it intends to treat SPARTA as a live enforcement tool, not a dead letter. On January 12, 2026, the FTC announced it's seeking information from 20 universities about whether sports agents working with student-athletes have complied with SPARTA's requirements.

The FTC's press release states three things plainly:

1. SPARTA requires disclosures to the athlete and notice to schools, including "specific language requirements" in a disclosure document.

2. Agents must notify the athlete's school within 72 hours after entering a contract (or before the athlete's next eligible athletic event, whichever is earlier).

3. The FTC's letters request information such as the date the school was notified, the agent's name, and whether complaints have been received, with responses requested by March 23, 2026.

This is not a theoretical future. It's happening now.

But this still doesn't solve the real problem. SPARTA is mainly a consumer-protection style statute focused on disclosures and deceptive recruiting conduct. Obviously addressing that conduct is important, but it's not sufficient for NIL/Rev-Share representation. SPARTA does not create a modern, industry-wide licensing system. It does not create uniform fee caps. It does not define the line between true NIL and salary-like compensation. It doesn't create standardized contract terms. It's more of a baseline, not a full professional-regulation regime. More is needed in order to properly protect college athletes from the unregulated agent.

<u>State law: UAAA/RUAAA exists — but states are not uniform in practice</u>

At the state level, a major "model law" addressing agents has been the Uniform Athlete Agents Act of 2000 ("UAAA") and its later updates (referred to as the Revised Uniform Athlete Agents Act in some states).

A model law is a draft statute created by experts, legal scholars, or organizations (the Uniform Law Commission drafted the UAAA and RUAAA) that serves as a template for a new law. It's designed to be adopted, in whole or part, by state or national legislatures to promote uniformity in the law and what the drafter of the law considers to be "best practices" across different jurisdictions.

The NCAA has long promoted the UAAA because it governs certain aspects of the agent-athlete-school relationship. For example, the original UAAA requires agent background information and includes a written notice requirement to institutions when a student-athlete signs an agency contract. The RUAAA (updated in 2019) expanded the definition of "athlete agent" as well as "student-athlete," allowed for reciprocal registration between the states, added new requirements for signing an agency contract, and expanded notification requirements. Currently, 42 states have adopted either the UAAA or the updated RUAAA.

But here's the problem for athletes and families: the laws regulating athlete agents are not the same in every state.

While the majority of states have adopted either the UAAA or the RUAAA, some key states (California, Michigan, and Ohio) have non-UAAA agency laws. And of the 42 states that have adopted the UAAA or RUAAA, those states have made their personal changes to the model laws. So the "uniform" law is not so uniform across the states.

Add into the mix the fact that there's also the NCAA NIL policy that must be followed, along with other emerging state NIL laws, as well as court cases flying off the presses, and this patchwork of policies, laws, and court orders becomes a legal minefield.

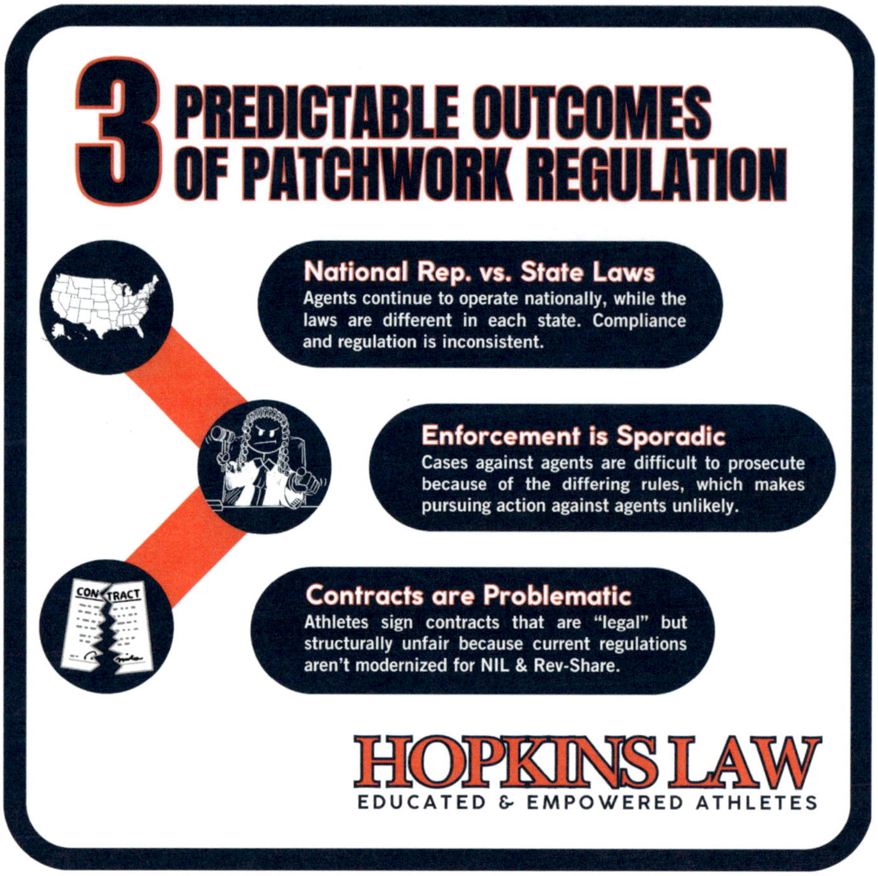

So yes, there *are* rules. But as a practical matter, the market is still operating without a unified, sports-industry standard for agent conduct and compensation that actually matches the NIL & Rev-Share world.

The Pricing Problem: Representation Fees Are All Over the Map

In the NIL era, agent representation is commonly priced as a percentage of athlete compensation. The problem in this new era is that there is no standardized percentage that agents are charging athletes for their representation. Some agents or sports agencies are charging upwards of "20% for NIL deals." The industry standard in the NFL is 3% of player contracts, and the NBA is 5% of player contracts.

The confusion comes in because the agents who represent NFL or NBA players also charge a higher percentage (10-20%) for endorsement (NIL) deals. Agents working with college athletes seem to charge only one price for their services, and that price is not standardized across the market.

Agents being paid a percentage of the contract value is normal, but in the current NIL/Rev-Share world, an important question needs to be asked in order to determine if the percentage is fair or not: What is the agent actually being paid on?

It's important to think of the money funding an athlete's contract as coming from one of two lanes: 1) the NIL lane; or, 2) the Rev-Share lane.

As we have discussed previously, NIL contracts cannot tie an athlete to a particular school. The use of an athlete's NIL is solely related to a legitimate business using the NIL of an athlete to promote a product or service, regardless of where the athlete is enrolled in school. The school is not a party to an NIL deal.

Rev-Share contracts are primarily used to secure an athlete's roster spot on a particular team. The school is the party to the contract, and pays the athletes to play a sport at the school. Some confusion may occur because those Rev-Share contracts also allow the schools to use the athlete's NIL (on ticket stubs, in advertising, etc.), but the language of the agreement requires the athlete to play at a specific school (something a pure NIL contract cannot do).

<u>NIL Contract Percentages</u>

If the payment under the contract is tied to marketing value (a brand endorsement, a licensing arrangement, a merchandise deal, appearances, deliverables), then a marketing-style commission makes sense because the agent is (at least in theory) creating and negotiating commercial value. That's called "sweat equity," where the agent is working hard to secure a brand deal on behalf of their client.

These contracts cannot require a player (either expressly or impliedly) to play for a particular school, and must follow all of the criteria under the House settlement to qualify as a true NIL deal.

If the deal is a true NIL deal, then it would be reasonable for the agent to charge 10-20% of the value of the contract for their services.

<u>Rev-Share Contract Percentages</u>

Rev-Share contracts are paid by the school and require an athlete to attend and play for their school. If the payment under the contract is tied to an athlete being on the team, then charging a marketing-style (NIL) commission is unreasonable.

Rev-Share contracts are similar to NFL or NBA player contracts (the contracts players sign to play for a particular team, such as TreVeyon Henderson's 4 year, $11,143,234 deal to play for the New England Patriots). The percentage an agent charges under a Rev-Share-style contract should be in the 3-5% range, not the 10-20% range.

The sources of payments to college athletes are anything but clear, unfortunately. Deals are labeled "NIL deals" but appear to require an athlete to play for a particular school. Such a clause in an "NIL deal" would convert the deal to a Rev-Share agreement (because only Rev-Share contracts can tie an athlete to a particular school).

Collective NIL Deals

Collectives are the entities that were formed at every major Division I school (following the 2021 Supreme Court decision in Alston) to pool money to pay players to play for a particular school.

Under the House settlement, deals made by the collectives are no longer allowed to be pay-for-play deals. Collectives are still pooling money to pay players, but they are rebranding the payments. Many collectives have filed for 501(c)(3) status and request donations from alumni and fans of a particular team. The collectives then pay athletes for what are essentially meet-and-greets and/or "work" at an animal shelter or hospital in the local area.

The collectives still serve as central, albeit sometimes controversial, drivers of NIL activity for a specific school, often influencing recruiting, transfer portal decisions, and team retention by providing high-value deals. The House settlement allowed these collectives to remain as a player in this new era.

If we're being honest, collective deals are NIL deals in name only. They still function as a supplement to any Rev-Share contract a college athlete signs. And if the contract is ultimately a Rev-Share contract, then the agent should charge the lower, 3-5%, commission.

But in today's market, agents representing college athletes typically charge just one percentage for all deals the athlete signs, and that percentage can be up to 20% (with one coach reporting an agent charged an athlete 30%). Deals need to be differentiated and the price an agent charges needs to correspond to the type of deal that is being signed, no matter how the deal is labeled. Deals that are labeled "NIL" even though the terms clearly reflect "Rev-Share" should be priced accordingly.

The Hopkins Law Fix: A Standard Athlete Representation Agreement With a Two-Lane Compensation Framework

My solution is simple: standardize the representation contract so the athlete begins from a fair default rather than a negotiation deficit. Terms are uniform, and agents will be forced to explain deviations.

I provide access to a standard athlete representation agreement through my website (hlosportslaw.com). The purpose is not to eliminate representation; it's to remove ambiguity and predatory pricing from the default structure, especially for athletes and families who don't have knowledgeable counsel at the negotiating table.

Lane One: Rev-Share Representation Fee = 3% (Fixed)

Rev-Share is your salary. The fairest analog in sports is the "player contract advisor" model where compensation is capped.

Separately from NIL, SPARTA already imposes a 72-hour notice concept and mandated disclosure language, which highlights that representation contracts in the student-athlete space are serious and eligibility-sensitive. But SPARTA does not set a fee rule, so athletes remain exposed to predatory agents.

My standard agreement addresses that exposure:

- If the money is Rev-Share (salary-like), the representative compensation is fixed at 3%.
- No "creative" re-labeling. No "success fee." No stacking of fees through affiliates.
- Why a fixed percentage? Because variable percentages invite manipulation and confusion.
- A fixed cap creates:
    - Transparency,
    - Comparability,
    - and a predictable market standard that schools and athletes can understand.

Athletes and families will have to be diligent in analyzing the deals athletes are signing to determine if the deal is an NIL deal or is more akin to Rev-Share (locking a player in on a specific roster).

Lane Two: True NIL Representation Fee = Professional Endorsement Benchmark

For true NIL deals (endorsement, licensing, and merchandise/marketing deals that are not player contracts) commission-based pricing is normal. The question is not whether a percentage exists; the question is whether the contract:

- clearly defines "true NIL,"
- limits scope creep,
- and prevents an agent from taking a marketing commission on salary-like money.

My standard agreement ties true NIL compensation to a professional endorsement/marketing benchmark -- not because the pro world is perfect, but because it is at least a mature market with understood norms and clearer role separation.

Contract provisions that make the fee framework enforceable (not just aspirational)

A fee clause is meaningless if the rest of the contract lets the representative re-label compensation or broaden scope indefinitely (scope creep). So the standard agreement will include:

- Definitions and classification controls
- "Rev-Share Compensation" vs. "True NIL Deal" defined in plain English.
- A classification clause: if compensation is primarily triggered by athletic participation/roster status, it is treated as Rev-Share for fee purposes—regardless of what the parties call it.
- Scope and minimum services
- Clear deliverables: negotiation, written term summaries, compliance reporting guidance, and documented communications.
- No vague "brand building" promises used to justify percentages.
- Term and termination protections
- Short initial term, athlete-friendly termination for cause.
- No post-termination "phantom commission" unless a specific deal was actually negotiated during the term.
- Conflict disclosures.
- Relationships with collectives, boosters, or affiliates must be disclosed.
- No undisclosed referral fees or fee-splitting.

Ensuring the contract has the above-referenced terms (and more) is how a contract becomes a protective instrument rather than a trap. You'll want to feel good about the deals that you are signing (NIL and Rev-Share), when you're signing them. To be educated about the different types of representation, and the various clauses that control different situations, will have you signing those deals with confidence instead of confusion.

Why Federal Regulation Is a Risky Fit -- and Why the Sports Should Self-Regulate

While a standardized contract will provide significant protection for athletes signing NIL and Rev-Share deals, more oversight of the entire landscape is desperately needed. And to be clear: the FTC's move discussed above *is* significant because it reinforces that the federal government is paying attention. The FTC has explicitly stated it is seeking information to understand whether agents are complying with SPARTA and whether student-athletes are being protected. The FTC has also publicly warned those who represent college athletes to comply with SPARTA.

But federal oversight comes with a fundamental limitation: the federal government enforces broad consumer-protection rules; it does not live inside the sports ecosystem. That matters because NIL/Rev-Share disputes are rarely just "consumer fraud." Most importantly, federal regulation of sports would be a bad idea. With the government's susceptibility to lobbyists and political maneuvering (and all the collateral damage that comes with it), Washington shouldn't be the referee for college athletics. It would amount to a failing product being managed by a failing system.

And as discussed previously, SPARTA is, by design, a baseline statute with a specific focus: unfair or deceptive practices, required disclosures, and notice. It doesn't create a comprehensive professional licensing, compensation, and discipline system. And that's what college sports needs, desperately.

The better model is to have college sports govern itself; have sports-industry regulation the way pro sports does it.

First, there needs to be a centralized certification process for all agents for college athletes. The NCAA or the CSC could operate that system, which would include a disciplinary process.

Right now, because of the flurry of lawsuits, with the NCAA being kicked around the courtroom, college sports feels like a free-for-all. It doesn't feel like there's a mom and dad enforcing the rules anymore. Now, it's more like a drunk uncle watching the kids, passed out on the couch. But that needs to stop. Agents need to submit to a certification process, and there needs to be disciplinary action against predatory agents.

Second, there should be universal, standardized agreements in college sports. That would include NIL deals, Rev-Share agreements, and agency contracts. The contracts need to have transparent fee limits, and clear, standard terms. Currently, conferences use standard agreements, but there should be one agreement for all college athletes (differentiated for each sport).

That's the model the NCAA (or an NCAA-aligned/College Sports Commission structure) is best positioned to implement because it can integrate:

- eligibility realities,
- compliance reporting,
- and the economic structure of Rev-Share.

In other words, the real solution isn't "more laws," it's the right regulator, using the right tools, with a modern understanding of the market.

The NIL/Rev-Share world is not going away. The money will keep growing, and representation will keep following it. The question is whether athletes will keep signing agreements where the fee structure is untethered from the true nature of the compensation, and the contract is written for the representative's flexibility rather than the athlete's protection.

My position is straightforward:

1. Rev-Share is salary-like. It should be priced like salary-like representation: 3%.

2. True NIL is commercial marketing (valid business purpose). It should be priced like commercial marketing, but only when it is genuinely "true NIL" and doesn't tie an athlete to a specific school.

3. The contract should be standard, transparent, and athlete-protective by default, not "negotiable" only for the small percentage of athletes who have sophisticated counsel.

Granted, to implement these changes, the NCAA will likely face lawsuits. That's because athletes have grown accustomed to challenging the NCAA's every move, and rightfully so. But these changes will easily hold up to legal scrutiny because they are changes that are for the best interest of the college athlete.

The End of
Module Five
ONWARD!! to MODULE SIX!!!
Let's Get Down to Business!

MODULE SIX

ESTABLISHING AND STRUCTURING YOUR NIL BUSINESS LEGALLY

Your first NIL payment hits your account on a Tuesday afternoon, and by Wednesday the bank is asking for a business name to keep deposits from being flagged; on Friday a brand emails a W-9; Saturday you sell a few dozen hoodies at a pop-up and someone asks for a receipt with sales tax; the next week your payment app freezes a payout "pending verification," and a month later a letter arrives from the IRS you don't quite understand. None of this is about ambition or talent -- it's about structure, and whether you built the necessary financial structure before the money started moving. Module Six guides you through establishing the legal and administrative framework for your NIL and Rev-Share ventures, including how to start a business that will help lay a solid foundation for all future financial activities. If you want payments to clear, taxes to be predictable, contracts to be enforceable, and your personal savings to stay protected, this is where that future is secured.

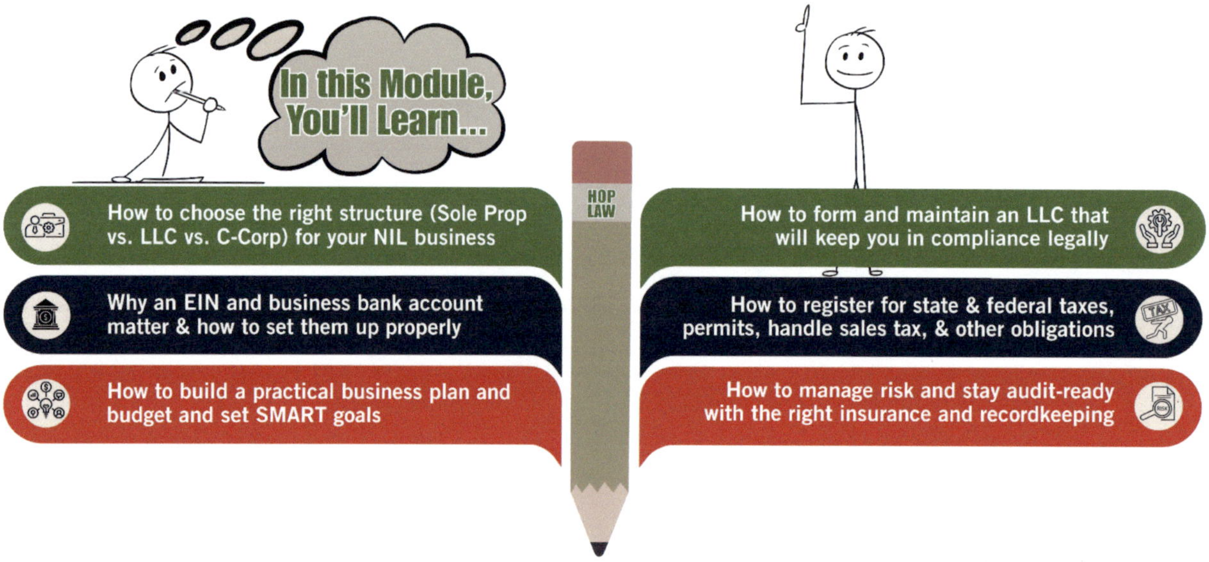

Choosing Your Business Structure: Sole Proprietorship vs. LLC vs. S-Corp -- Pros and Cons

The first time you accept money from a person or business to use your name, image, or likeness, you've started a business. You may not recognize it as a business and just deposit the money in the bank or spend it when you get it, but by accepting money in exchange for your NIL, you are now a business. While you may not have knowingly chosen to start a business, choosing the right business structure is one of the most important financial decisions you'll make.

The business structure you choose will impact your taxes, legal risk, paperwork, and growth potential. We'll do a deep dive into the main options -- Sole Proprietorship, LLC, and C-Corps -- so you can make the smartest choice for your brand, your money, and your future.

Sole Proprietorship

A sole proprietorship is the simplest way to start a business. As soon as you start earning income as a college athlete (through NIL deals, appearances, merch, etc.) without forming a legal entity, you are considered a sole proprietor by default.

Pros:

- Easy & inexpensive: No formal paperwork needed to start -- just begin business activities.
- Full control: You're the boss and make all decisions.
- Simple taxes: All income and expenses are reported directly on your personal tax return (Schedule C).

Cons:

- Unlimited personal liability: You are personally responsible for all business debts or legal issues. If something goes wrong, your personal assets (bank accounts, car, etc.) are at risk, meaning you'll have to use those assets to pay debts.
- Harder to separate finances: Business and personal money can get mixed, making tracking the money and paying taxes accurately more challenging.

- ❖ Limited credibility: Some partners, sponsors, or brands may prefer to work with an established entity for professionalism and legal reasons.

Limited Liability Company

A Limited Liability Company (LLC) is the most popular choice for small businesses and athletes. An LLC is an official legal entity created in your state that protects your personal assets from business risks and lawsuits.

Pros:

- ❖ Liability protection: Your personal assets are shielded from most business debts or lawsuits, as long as you keep your business separated and stay compliant.
- ❖ Flexible management: You can run your LLC alone (single-member) or with partners (multi-member) without much red tape.
- ❖ Simple tax options: By default, a one-person LLC is taxed just like a sole proprietorship (with pass-through taxation), but you can choose to be taxed as an S-Corp (explained later) if it benefits you.
- ❖ Professionalism: Having "LLC" after your business name adds credibility with sponsors, partners, and banks.

Cons:

- ❖ Cost to create: There are state filing fees ($50–$500+) and annual reporting fees to keep your LLC in good standing.
- ❖ Ongoing paperwork: You must file paperwork each year, keep business and personal finances separate, and appoint a registered agent for service of process (getting served with official notices).

If you decide to close your LLC, you must formally dissolve it with your state. Not doing so may lead to fines or create risks of identity theft.

Corporation

A "C" Corporation (C-Corp) is a distinct legal entity separate from its owners, offering the strongest personal liability protection of the three options. They come in different forms, including standard C-corps and S-corps, with S-corps offering pass-through taxation to avoid double taxation.

Pros:

- Limited liability protection: The corporation is a separate legal entity, so shareholders' personal assets are generally shielded from corporate debts and lawsuits. If you co-mingle personal and business assets, that could be grounds to "pierce the corporate veil." Piercing the corporate veil is a legal action where a court disregards the limited liability of a corporation or LLC and holds its owners personally responsible for the company's debts and obligations.
- Growth & capital flexibility: Can issue multiple classes of stock, have unlimited shareholders, and attract outside investors more easily than pass-through entities.
- Perpetual existence: The corporation continues even if shareholders or management change or leave.
- Fringe benefit and deductions: Can deduct benefits (health insurance, retirement contributions) for employees/shareholders and potentially use retained earnings for reinvestment.

Cons:

- Double taxation: Profits are taxed at the corporate level, and then dividends or distributions to shareholders are taxed again at the individual level.
- Compliance burden & complexity: More formal requirements (board meetings, bylaws, minutes, reporting) and administrative overhead.
- Losses don't pass through: Losses at the corporate level typically cannot be used to offset personal income of shareholders.
- Higher operational costs: Legal, accounting, regulatory, and administrative costs tend to be higher.

S-Election Explained:

An S-election is a tax status a corporation (or LLC) can choose with the IRS to avoid being taxed twice. Instead of the business paying corporate taxes, the profits "pass through" to the owner's personal tax return.

- Taking an S-election is not always worth it for small earnings: The tax savings usually become worth it only if your business consistently makes $30,000–$50,000 or more in profit each year after expenses.

THE FINE PRINT: S-Election for C-Corps & LLCs

Pass-Through Taxation:
Profits, losses, deductions, and credits flow through to your personal tax return, avoiding corporate-level "double taxation."

Reduced Self-Employment Tax:
Only your salary is subject to FICA (Social Security & Medicare); additional distributions (if permitted) may avoid those payroll taxes.

Liability Protection:
You get the protections of a corporate structure (your personal assets are generally shielded from business debts) while enjoying tax benefits.

Flexibility & Credibility:
Easy to transfer ownership, and having a corporation adds professionalism with investors, partners, and brands.

Example Scenario:
Suppose you form a corporation for your athlete brand and elect S status. Your business earns $100,000 net in a year.

You decide to pay yourself a salary of $40,000 (subject to employment taxes).

The remaining $60,000 is distributed to you as "dividends / distributions," which are not subject to self-employment tax (though you still report them as income).

You avoid paying corporate income tax at the entity level; your total tax burden is on your individual return.

How to Choose: Key Questions

? **How much risk does your NIL business carry?** (If you're doing public appearances, endorsements, or anything with risk, the liability protection of an LLC or S-Corp is invaluable.)

? **How much money do you expect to make?** (If it's small and infrequent, starting as a sole proprietor can be simplest; for larger or growing earnings, consider forming an LLC or S-Corp.)

? **Do you want to work with others?** (An LLC or S-Corp can support multiple owners, while a sole proprietorship cannot.)

? **Are you ready for more paperwork?** (LLCs and especially S-Corps require more setup, accounting, and compliance.)

? **Will you reinvest or scale your business?** (Entities like LLC and S-Corp offer more flexibility for future growth.)

Wrap Up:

Sole Proprietorship: Easy, low-cost, but offers no personal liability protection.

LLC: Best balance of simplicity, flexibility, liability protection, and professionalism for most athletes' businesses.

Corporation (C-Corp): Offers strong liability protection and growth potential, but comes with double taxation and more complexity.

S-Corp: Advanced tax strategy for bigger profits, but brings more rules and paperwork.

Choosing the right structure is the first step to running a successful, sustainable business as a college athlete. Take your time, review the options, and seek advice from a professional if you're unsure. Making the right choice now can save you money, stress, and risk as you build your brand and secure your future.

How To Form An LLC (Step-by-Step Guidance)

Establishing an LLC is a powerful move for college athletes because it gives you legal protection, keeps your business professional, and sets you up for success as your NIL opportunities grow. Here's a detailed, step-by-step guide to forming your LLC and key points to keep in mind as a college athlete:

1. Pick a Unique Business Name
Your business name must be unique and follow your state's naming rules (usually it must include "LLC" or a similar phrase).

Use your Secretary of State's website to search name availability. Make sure not to skip this, as duplicate names are not allowed.

Consider branding: make sure your name matches the image you want to present. You'll also want to check to see if your business name (or a variation) is available as a domain name if you're going to also start a website.

2. Choose Your Formation State
You can form your LLC in any state, but it's usually best to pick the state where you go to school or expect to do most business.

Forming out-of-state may require paying for a registered agent (for service of process (serving legal documents on the business)) and foreign registration fees. Most large businesses choose to incorporate in Delaware because of the friendly tax scheme the state has for businesses. Other businesses choose Nevada, as it's called "the Delaware of the West."

This is a more broad consideration that isn't necessarily vital to the success of your business, but if you want to be thorough in your business set up, it should be a consideration.

3. Designate a Registered Agent
Every LLC must have a registered agent with a physical address in the state of formation.

The registered agent receives legal/official mail on your company's behalf. You can be your own agent if you live in-state, or hire a service if not.

It's easiest to be your own registered agent, but keep in mind that the registered agent has to have a physical address (not a P.O. Box). So if you don't have an office and don't want to give out your personal home address, you may want to consider hiring a service that acts as a company's registered agent.

4. Prepare and File "Articles of Organization"
This is the key legal document officially creating your LLC. In the Articles, you'll list:

- The LLC's name
- The principal (business) address
- Registered agent's name and address
- Purpose of the business (can be broad, e.g., "engaging in all lawful business activities")
- Members/managers names and addresses

File the Articles online or by mail with the Secretary of State. The filing fee usually ranges from $50–$500, depending on the state.

<u>Example (Sample Key Sections)</u>:

Article 1. Name: Tiger Athlete Ventures, LLC
Article 2. Principal Address: 123 College Blvd, Campus City, State Zip

Article 3. Registered Agent: Sam Student, 123 College Blvd, Campus City, State Zip
Article 4. Purpose: To engage in athlete brand promotion, appearances, and related business activities.
Article 5. Organizer Signature: Sam Student, 10/5/2025

5. Create an LLC Operating Agreement (Recommended)
An LLC Operating Agreement is essential even if your state doesn't require it. This internal document defines who owns what percentage of the business, how key decisions get made, how profits and losses are split, and what happens if an owner wants out or if the business dissolves. It protects all members by setting clear expectations upfront and reducing the chances of confusion or legal disputes later, especially critical when you have partners.

This private document lays out (among anything else you feel is important):

- ❖ Who owns how much of the business.
- ❖ How decisions are made and by whom.
- ❖ How profits/losses are shared.
- ❖ What happens if someone leaves the business.

6. Get an Employer Identification Number (EIN)
An EIN is like a "Social Security number" for your business. Just like your Social Security number, your business's EIN is a nine-digit number. You'll use the EIN for everything associated with the business, including opening a bank account, obtaining business cell phones, hiring people, receiving money, paying taxes, and anything else with the IRS.

If you're reading this as part of a Hopkins Law Sports Management workshop, you'll be able to apply for and obtain your business's EIN today. See a detailed explanation below as to how to obtain one.

7. Register with State Tax & Local Licenses (if needed)
If you sell merchandise or offer taxable services, register for state sales tax permits. Some states or cities may require additional business licenses. Check with your local (city or county) government for any license requirements.

8. Open a Business Bank Account
Open a business bank account using your LLC documents and EIN to keep your business and personal finances separate. This separation is crucial for maintaining your liability protection because if you mix funds, courts could "pierce the corporate veil" and hold you personally responsible for business debts. One of the main reasons to create a business is to

protect your personal assets; if you treat your business account/money as your personal money, then your personal assets are no longer protected by the corporation (because there is no distinction between your personal and business assets).

Your business should pay you just like it would any other vendor or employee, not share an account with you. That means you either pay yourself a regular physical paycheck each month, or you transfer money from your business bank account into your personal bank account with a note indicating the payment is for your paycheck. Keeping clean records makes taxes, accounting, and your life much easier, especially if you get audited or sued.

9. Maintain Your LLC

Maintaining your LLC is about keeping it legally active and in good standing. Most states require you to file an annual or biennial report; miss that and your LLC could be suspended. I know I just warned you, but it bears repeating: you also need to keep your business finances and records completely separate from your personal ones to preserve your liability protection. Anytime your address, ownership, or registered agent changes, make sure to update your state filings right away. Staying on top of these basics helps ensure your LLC continues to protect you.

HOP LAW Insight:

Age Restrictions: Some states require LLC members to be 18+. If you're underage, discuss options with a legal advisor.

Compliance: Always keep on top of paperwork and deadlines to protect your liability shield.

Professionalism: Use your LLC for all NIL, endorsement, and related business contracts and not your personal name. Any check you receive as payment should only have your business name on it, not your personal name.

Long-Term Planning: An LLC makes it easier to scale your ventures, bring in partners, and transition from athlete to entrepreneur.

Setting up an LLC is a critical first step in treating yourself like the business you are. It's not overly complicated, but it does require careful attention to detail and state requirements. Once you start running the business, you'll have routine operations that will start to feel like second nature to you, like your free throw routine.

When in doubt, consult your campus resources, a legal advisor, or a trusted financial professional (preferably a CPA) to walk you through the process.

Obtaining Your EIN (Employer Identification Number)

As explained above, your business's EIN is like a Social Security number for your business. As a review here's why you need an EIN:

- ❖ Open a business bank account in your LLC's name.
- ❖ Keep business and personal finances separate, protecting your liability shield.
- ❖ Report your income and pay taxes as a business, not just as an individual.
- ❖ Hire employees or independent contractors (if your business grows).
- ❖ Sign contracts and invoice companies or sponsors professionally.

Step-by-Step: How to Get Your EIN

1. Form Your LLC or Business First
Before applying, make sure you have officially registered your LLC or other business entity with your state. The IRS will ask for these details. Applying before your entity is formed can cause delays.

2. Gather Needed Information

- ❖ Your legal business name (exactly as filed with the state)
- ❖ Business address (usually your campus or primary business location)
- ❖ Name and Social Security Number (SSN) or Individual Taxpayer Identification Number (ITIN) for the "responsible party" (usually you!)
- ❖ Reason for applying (select "Started a new business")

3. Apply Online (Recommended for U.S. Applicants)

- ❖ Go to the IRS EIN Assistant: irs.gov/EIN
- ❖ The application is available Monday–Friday, 7 a.m.–10 p.m. Eastern.
- ❖ Complete the process in one sitting -- no saves! Print or save your confirmation letter.

You'll get your EIN immediately. This is the number you can use right away to open a bank account and conduct business.

4. Alternative: Apply by Fax or Mail

- ❖ Print Form SS-4 (Application for Employer Identification Number) from the IRS website.
- ❖ Fill out the form using your business information.
- ❖ Fax to 855-641-6935 if you want your EIN in about 4 business days.

- ❖ Or mail to: Internal Revenue Service, Attn: EIN Operation, Cincinnati, OH 45999 (receive your EIN by mail in about 4 weeks).
- ❖ International applicants can apply by phone or fax using the contacts on the IRS website.

Quick Form SS-4 Walkthrough (Key Lines):

Line 1. Legal name of LLC

Line 2. Trade name (if different)

Line 3. Name of responsible party (often you)

Line 4. Business address

Line 8. Specify LLC (if that's your choice); enter formation date (month, year)

Line 10. Reason for applying ("Started a new business")

Line 18. Third-party designee (leave blank unless someone else applies for you)

Sign and date the bottom of the form (you, as owner or manager).

HOP LAW Insight:

One EIN per entity per day: The IRS assigns only one EIN per responsible party per day, so plan ahead if you're juggling multiple businesses.

International students: If you don't have an SSN, you may need to apply for an ITIN before requesting an EIN. Check your visa and work eligibility status, and get campus or legal help if needed.

Keep your EIN safe: Print the confirmation, and store it with your most important documents. You'll use this for every official business, bank, or tax transaction.

Beware of scams: Never pay to apply for an EIN; it's 100% free with the IRS. Avoid third-party websites that charge for this service.

Update changes promptly: If your address or responsible party changes, file IRS Form 8822-B within 60 days to stay compliant.

Securing your EIN is a rite of passage in your journey as an athlete-entrepreneur. With this number in hand, you're ready to open business accounts, sign deals, and keep your NIL or Rev-Share money organized and secure. If you hit a snag, don't hesitate to seek help from a campus advisor or a trusted legal or financial professional. But setting your business structure up right from the start will serve you now and for years to come.

Opening A Business Bank Account (Step-by-Step)

Opening a dedicated business bank account is a critical step for managing your NIL and Rev-Share earnings professionally and protecting your personal finances. A separate account helps simplify bookkeeping, maintain liability protections, and build credibility with sponsors and partners. Here's a clear, step-by-step guide to opening your account, plus a handy checklist of what you'll need.

Step-by-Step Process

1. Consider the Type of Bank to Work With
Not all banks are the same. It's important to research banks, from big, national banks, to local credit unions. Think about convenience/location, fees, account features, and digital banking options.

Also, look for accounts designed for small businesses with no or low fees for the services that matter to you.

2. Gather Required Documents
Most banks require several documents to open a business account. Prepare these ahead of time:

<u>Business Formation Documents</u>: LLC Articles of Organization or Certificate of Formation

<u>EIN</u>: Your Employer Identification Number from the IRS

<u>Operating Agreement</u>: Defines ownership and management (especially for multi-member LLCs)

<u>Personal Identification</u>: Valid government-issued ID (driver's license, passport)

<u>Resolution to Open Account</u>: If your LLC has multiplc members, you may need a document authorizing you to open the account

3. Visit the Bank or Apply Online
Many banks allow online applications, but some require an in-person visit.

Bring all documents and identification with you.

Complete the application with accurate business information.

It's preferred to open your business bank account in-person so that any issues can be worked out immediately. You'll likely have questions about different banking options the bank offers, or any number of other questions that may arise, and it would be more efficient to have those questions answered by a real person and not a chatbot.

4. Fund Your Account
Deposit the minimum opening balance, typically $25–$100.

5. Order Checks and Cards
Request business checks and debit/credit cards for managing expenses. The checks and debit/credit cards are the tools necessary for keeping your business expenses separate from your personal expenses. If you go out to eat and it's dinner with friends, you'd pay with your personal credit card. If you are at a restaurant for a business meeting regarding a potential NIL deal or with your business partners, then you would pay with your business card, keep the receipt, and log it into your expense tracking software.

Having separate checks and debit/credit cards is essential for maintaining a clear division between your business and personal expenses.

6. Set Up Online Banking
Enroll in online banking, mobile apps, and automatic alerts. Having online banking through your phone is vital to keeping you informed about the status of your account at a moment's notice. It'll also be more convenient to deposit checks, transfer money, or anything else that you need done without visiting a bank.

7. Keep Account Information Secure
Store checks, cards, and login credentials safely. This should go without stating, but make sure to protect your finances as best you can. This could include having a safe at your home or business, using password apps, having two-factor authentication, and using an identity theft wallet (called RFID blocking wallets).

Opening a business bank account is more than just a formality, it's a cornerstone of managing your financial future with discipline and professionalism. Take your time, prepare your documents, and make sure you choose a banking partner that supports your goals as a student-athlete and entrepreneur.

Registering For State Taxes And Sales Permits

If you're selling merchandise, offering taxable services, or earning income from NIL and Rev-Share opportunities, you may need to register for state taxes or obtain a sales permit. You'll have to register with your state to pay taxes. This process ensures you comply with state laws, avoid penalties, and professionally run your business. Here's how to navigate these steps, with a spotlight on what to do in California as an example.

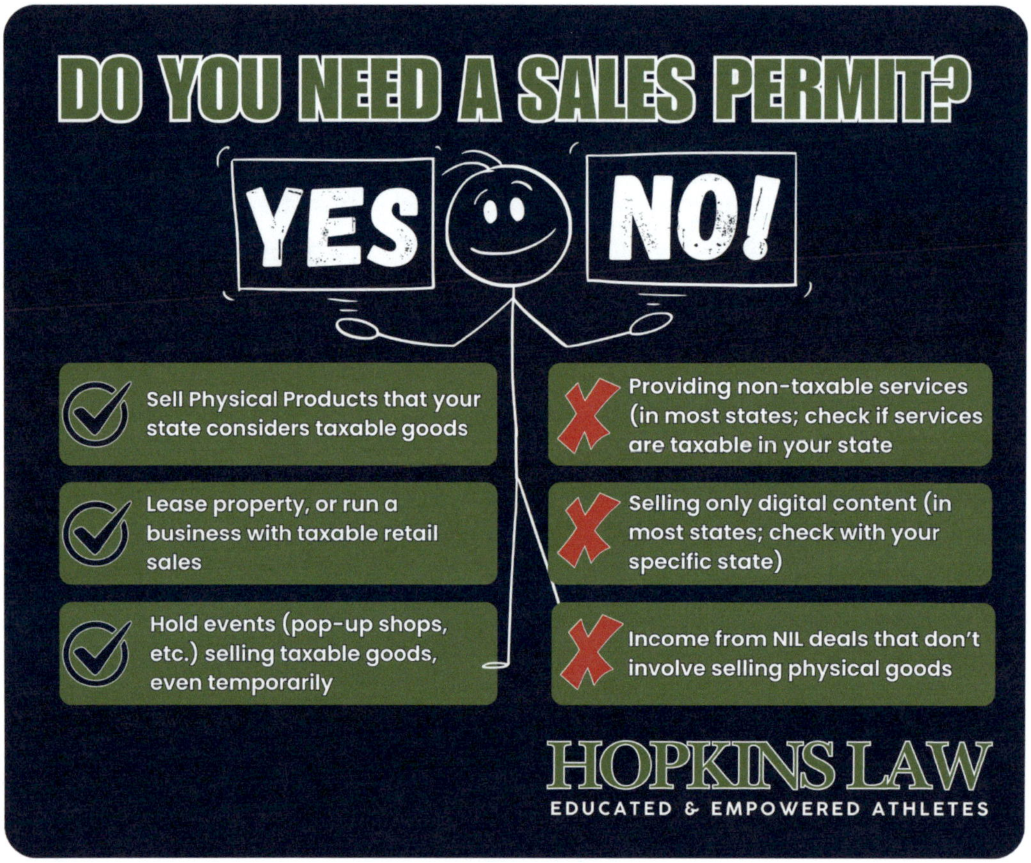

Step-by-Step: How to Register for State Taxes and Sales Permits (California Example)

1. Gather Your Information

Before you start, have these ready:

- ❖ Your LLC paperwork
- ❖ Your EIN (Employer Identification Number)

- ❖ Your business address and/or place of operations
- ❖ Expected monthly or annual sales, including taxable vs. non-taxable sales
- ❖ Details of suppliers and bank accounts
- ❖ Your SSN, driver's license/state ID, and contact info

2. Apply Online

California: Go to cdtfa.ca.gov and click "Permits & Licenses" > "Register Online".

Answer the questions re: your business type, location, expected sales, and products sold.

If you sell physical items for less than 90 days (such as a pop-up event), request a temporary seller's permit.

Include information about suppliers and where you keep business records.

3. Report and Remit Sales Tax

Once you've registered, collect sales tax from customers at the time of sale (current rate in California varies by city/county).

File sales tax returns with the state on a regular basis (monthly, quarterly, or annually -- frequency depends on sales volume).

Pay the tax collected to the state according to deadlines.

4. Register for Additional State Accounts

If your business will have employees, register for state withholding and unemployment accounts as prompted during the process.

State Income Taxes and Multiple-State Filing

Track all states where you earn NIL income (including appearances, games, merchandise sales), as you may owe income tax both where you live and where you do business.

Understand residency rules: If you attend school out-of-state, you may owe filing in both your home state and your college state.

Nonresident states may tax a portion of your income based on where you participate in sports/events.

Important Note:
Not all states require sales permits, and some (e.g., Alaska, Delaware, Montana, New Hampshire, Oregon) do not have state sales tax. Check your state's business portal for requirements before selling products.

THE FINE PRINT: Protect the Bag — Legally

- Keep business and personal finances separate for clarity and compliance.
- Record all sales and sales tax collected for accurate reporting.
- If your NIL activities cross state lines, seek professional tax help to understand filing obligations and minimize surprises.
- Always check your local/campus compliance office or a NIL/Rev-Share competent lawyer for guidance on state-specific rules.
- Never skip state filings; penalties for late registration or unremitted taxes can be steep.
- Obtaining the proper permits and registering for state taxes is an essential part of running your NIL or Rev-Share business professionally, keeping you in good standing with the law, and the right side of your financial future.

When in doubt, consult a CPA!

How To Write A Successful Business Plan – Goal Setting And Strategy –

Writing a business plan isn't just for big companies; it's a smart tool for any business owner wanting a clear path as to how their business will operate and the plan for success. This is especially true for college athletes looking to likely start their first business with NIL or Rev-Share ventures.

Your business plan acts as your personal and professional roadmap, helping you clarify goals, set your strategy, and run your athlete brand like a business. Here's how to make a practical, actionable plan, plus why it pays off in the long run.

1. Set Clear Goals (SMART Goals)
Define exactly what you want to accomplish through your NIL and business activities. The best way to do this is with SMART goals: Specific, Measurable, Achievable, Relevant, and Time-bound. We'll get to how to obtain the goals in a minute.

<u>Examples</u>:

- "Secure 3 endorsement deals by end of spring semester."
- "Earn $15,000 from merchandise sales this academic year."
- "Grow my Instagram audience by 50% in 12 months."

Clarity here gives your business direction and motivates you to take actionable steps.

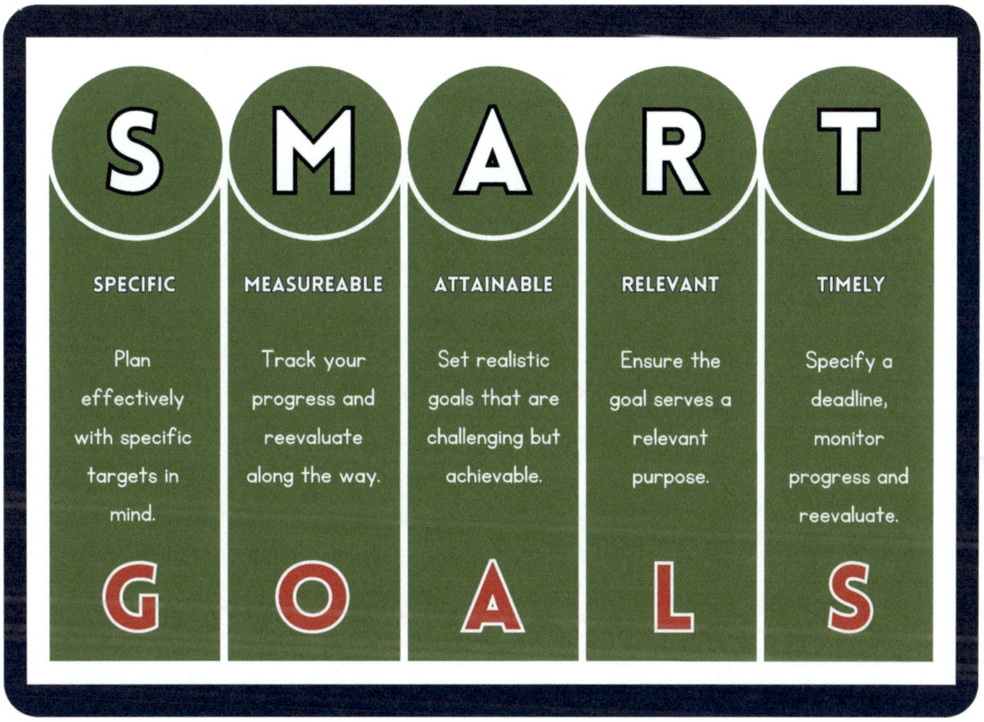

2. Identify Your Brand and Audience
Outline what makes your personal brand stand out and determine who you want to reach (fans, sponsors, local businesses, etc.). Think about your story, values, strengths, and what separates you from others in your sport.

- What do you want to be known for?
- Who is most interested in what you offer?
- What platforms will you use to connect with them?

Understanding your audience helps you tailor your strategy and find the best business opportunities.

3. Analyze the Market and Competition

Take time to research the NIL landscape for athletes like you. Who are your main competitors? What NIL deals are available in your local, regional, or sport-specific market? Identify ideal business partners and how you can bring them unique value.

- Look at what other athletes are doing successfully.
- Determine gaps where you can stand out.
- Make a short list of local businesses or brands you'd like to work with.

4. Outline Your Marketing and Outreach Strategy

Create a plan for how you'll promote your brand and connect with new partners. Storytelling is the best marketing strategy to promote your brand. People will be able to relate to your story, so long as it's authentic and relatable.

- Social media plan (content, frequency, audience engagement)
- Partnerships/collaborations (brands, collectives, other athletes)
- In-person events, appearances, or community involvement
- Website or digital presence

A clear marketing strategy helps you consistently build your brand, attract deals, and maintain authenticity.

5. Develop a Financial Plan and Budget

List all your expected income sources (endorsements, appearances, merch, etc.) and estimate business expenses (marketing, taxes, equipment, travel).

- Create a monthly or annual budget -- be realistic about income and costs
- Project your potential earnings
- Identify how much you'll need to save for taxes and future growth

Use spreadsheets or financial apps to track progress, or rely on a template for easy updates.

6. Create an Action Plan

Break bigger goals into smaller, manageable tasks so running your business or brand doesn't feel overwhelming. Creating an action plan helps you stay focused on what matters most, whether it's landing an NIL deal, building a social media presence, or launching a merch line. Ask yourself:

❖ What will you focus on each week or month?
❖ Who will you contact for support or partnerships?
❖ What deadlines will you set for new initiatives?

Put these answers into a timeline so you can track your growth. Regular check-ins keep you accountable, help you adapt when needed, and make your progress visible and motivating.

Put Together A Solid Team

A solid business plan includes the people you'll need to execute it. Identify the roles you can't (or shouldn't) do alone -- attorney, CPA/tax pro, marketing/brand lead, insurance broker, and a primary banker -- and plug those into your plan with clear responsibilities, timelines, and fees. Budget for professional help the same way you budget for equipment; it's a cost of doing business that reduces risk and saves money long-term. Finally, set a standing check-in cadence (monthly or quarterly) so your team is aligned and your plan stays on track as your goals evolve.

Goal Setting Action Plan

Business Name	Date:

In-Season Goal

What's My Why?

Potential Challenges to Achieve the Goal	Possible Solutions

How I WILL Invoke the Discipline Needed	How I Will Hold Myself Accountable

Tasks That Will Make Me Achieve My Goal

Date Done By:	Tasks	✓

7. Track Results & Adapt
A good business plan isn't set in stone. Review your goals, results, and strategies regularly. Adjust your action steps if you're not seeing the progress you want. Remember: you're the CEO of your athlete business so you have total control over every aspect of the business. It's important to routinely review what's working and what isn't and be ready to pivot.

HOP LAW Insight:

- Keep your plan short (1-3 pages is enough), and update as you grow.
- Use your business plan to pitch sponsors, track performance, and guide your decisions.
- Seek feedback from mentors, compliance officers, or business advisors so you can make pinpoint changes to your business plan and action steps.

With a focused plan, you'll be ready to set goals, take action, and maximize both your earning power and your business's likelihood of success.

Understanding Business Insurance Basics

Insurance may be a boring topic, but it's a vital one. Maximizing the protection of your business is equally as important as building your brand and business. Business insurance is a necessary tool that helps shield you from unexpected risks -- everything from liability claims to health-related issues -- that could otherwise derail your progress. This section breaks down essential types of insurance every athlete-entrepreneur should understand and consider obtaining.

1. General Liability Insurance
This coverage protects you if someone is injured or their property is damaged because of your business activities. For example, if you host a paid event or sell merchandise and a customer is harmed or experiences loss, liability insurance can cover legal fees and damages.

<u>Why It Matters</u>: Protects your personal and business assets if you are sued.

<u>When Needed</u>: If you hold public appearances, camps, sell products, or have regular interaction with customers.

2. Professional Liability Insurance (Errors & Omissions)
Also known as E&O insurance, this protects you if a client claims you gave bad advice or your services caused them harm or financial loss.

Why It Matters: Especially relevant if you provide coaching, training, consulting, or any guidance.

When Needed: If you coach others or offer paid expertise beyond athletic performance.

3. Health and Disability Insurance
While your school may provide basic health coverage, additional insurance can help cover injuries that affect your ability to compete or work.

Health Insurance: Ensure you have coverage beyond school-provided plans to protect against unexpected medical bills.

Disability Insurance: Provides income replacement if an injury or illness prevents you from earning money, including from NIL, sports, or business activities.

4. Property Insurance
If you sell merchandise or store valuable equipment (cameras, computers, uniforms), property

insurance protects you against loss or damage.

5. Cyber Liability Insurance
For athletes with an online business or selling digital products, this insurance covers data breaches or cyberattacks.

Why Insurance Matters for College Athletes

Injuries or business mishaps can happen unexpectedly. Insurance is not just about compliance or paperwork -- it's about peace of mind, financial security, and protecting the brand and business you're working hard to build. Taking proactive steps now can save you from costly setbacks later.

Remember, insurance needs grow as your business grows. Revisit your coverage regularly and update it as your NIL and entrepreneurial activities expand.

Having the right insurance coverage is a cornerstone of running a responsible, professional NIL or athlete business. It lets you focus on what matters most: your athletic performance and building your legacy and brand on your terms.

Business Record Retention & Compliance Tips

Interacting with the IRS is never fun. It's even less fun if the IRS chooses to audit you and your business. Maintaining organized and secure records is essential, not only for running a successful business, but also for making your business audit-proof.

THE FINE PRINT: What's An IRS Audit?

An IRS audit is when the IRS reviews your tax return to make sure your income, deductions, and expenses are accurate. It's like getting your financial game film reviewed — they're checking for mistakes or mishaps.

WHY IT HAPPENS:

- You didn't report all your income (like NIL money or Rev-Share payments).
- You claimed big deductions or business expenses that seem unusual.
- You filed late or had inconsistent info from year to year.

HOW TO PROTECT YOURSELF:

- Keep clean records — track every payment, invoice, and expense.
- Separate business and personal finances.
- File on time and report every dollar of income.

Audits are rare, but if one comes, you want to be ready. Think of it as another reason to run your NIL and rev-share business like a pro.

Proper record retention facilitates compliance with legal, tax, and operational requirements, and it ensures that you'll survive any audit. Proper organization also bullet-proofs you if you are sued or involved in any other disputes.

Here's a comprehensive guide to best practices:

1. Develop a Record Retention System

Create a Transparent Policy: Establish clear rules on how long different types of documents should be kept, where they are stored, and who has access.

Categorize Records: Group documents into categories such as contracts, financial records, tax documents, legal correspondence, and business licenses.

Set a Calendar for Review: Regularly review retained documents -- annually or biannually -- to determine if they should be retained, archived, or destroyed.

2. Maintain Secure Storage

Physical Storage: Use lockable file cabinets or safes for sensitive paper documents (contracts, legal papers, etc.). Ensure storage is in a safe, fireproof, and pest-resistant location.

Digital Storage: Use encrypted cloud-based platforms or secure servers for electronic files. Regularly back up digital records and use strong, unique passwords.

Access Control: Limit access to essential personnel or yourself. Keep an updated log of who has accessed or modified records.

3. Follow Legal and Tax Retention Requirements

Contracts & Legal Documents: Retain for the duration of your business activity plus at least 6 years, sometimes longer if advised. For example, California requires health records to be kept for at least 7 years after the last treatment, but some health records (Medi-Cal) are required to be kept for 10 years after last treatment.

Financial & Tax Records: Keep all invoices, receipts, bank statements, and tax filings (W-9s, 1099s, etc.) typically for at least 3-7 years, depending on the state; it's advisable to keep your tax returns indefinitely in electronic format.

Employment & Personnel Records: If applicable, keep for the length of employment plus several years (California law specifies 4 years for certain documents).

4. Protect Sensitive Data

Data Security: Use encryption, firewalls, and secure access controls to protect sensitive personal, legal, and financial information.

Physical Security: Store paper records in locked, access-controlled environments.

Employee & Contractor Data: Maintain confidentiality and limit access to only those who need it.

5. Implement Destruction Policies

Timely Disposal: Shred physical documents once retention periods expire. Delete electronic records securely by permanently removing files from servers, ensuring they cannot be recovered.

Document a Disposal Schedule: Keep a log of what is destroyed, when, and by whom to meet audit standards.

Secure Disposal Methods: Use certified shredding services for paper and reputable data destruction tools for digital files.

6. Use Technology Effectively

Record Management Software: Invest in platforms designed for secure document management and compliance tracking.

Automated Reminders: Set alerts for review and destruction dates.

Scan & Digitize: Convert physical documents to secure digital copies for easier access and safekeeping. Keep original paper copies only as long as legally required.

7. Regular Training and Audits

Staff Training: Educate yourself or your team on proper record-keeping protocols.

Periodic Audits: Regularly audit your records to ensure completeness, security, and compliance.

Review Policies: Update your retention policies when laws or business operations change.

8. Stay Informed About Local Regulations

Laws vary by state. Regularly review your state's requirements (e.g., California, Illinois, Georgia, etc.) or specific organizational policies. Consult legal counsel for complex situations, especially when dealing with sensitive medical, legal, or tax documents.

Proper record retention is not just about compliance, it's about safeguarding your business, ensuring accountability, and enabling easy access when you need it. Establish a clear system, secure your documents, follow legal timelines, and regularly review your procedures to stay audit-ready and compliant. By implementing these best practices, you'll protect your brand, be prepared for audits, and set a strong foundation for your athlete-entrepreneur journey.

MODULE SEVEN

BUILD A MONEY MANAGEMENT SYSTEM DESIGNED FOR SUCCESS

Now that you have your business set up with your entity chosen (Sole Prop/LLC/C-Corp), EIN in hand, operating agreement drafted, a dedicated bank account opened, and are protected with the right insurance plan, you're ready for that first check to come in. Before you start moving money through your business, we need to build a polished, repeatable system to track every dollar and deliverable. This module turns that foundation into daily habits: logging income and non-cash perks the moment they arrive, matching payments to contracts and invoices, reconciling your business account, saving for taxes, and organizing documents so your school, your CPA, and (if needed) an auditor can follow the story in minutes. The goal is simple: no scrambles, no surprises, just a clear record that protects your eligibility, your money, and your time. So when that first payment arrives, either as a mix of direct deposits, PayPal transfers, or a box of free gear, you won't panic, you'll rely on the system we're about to set up.

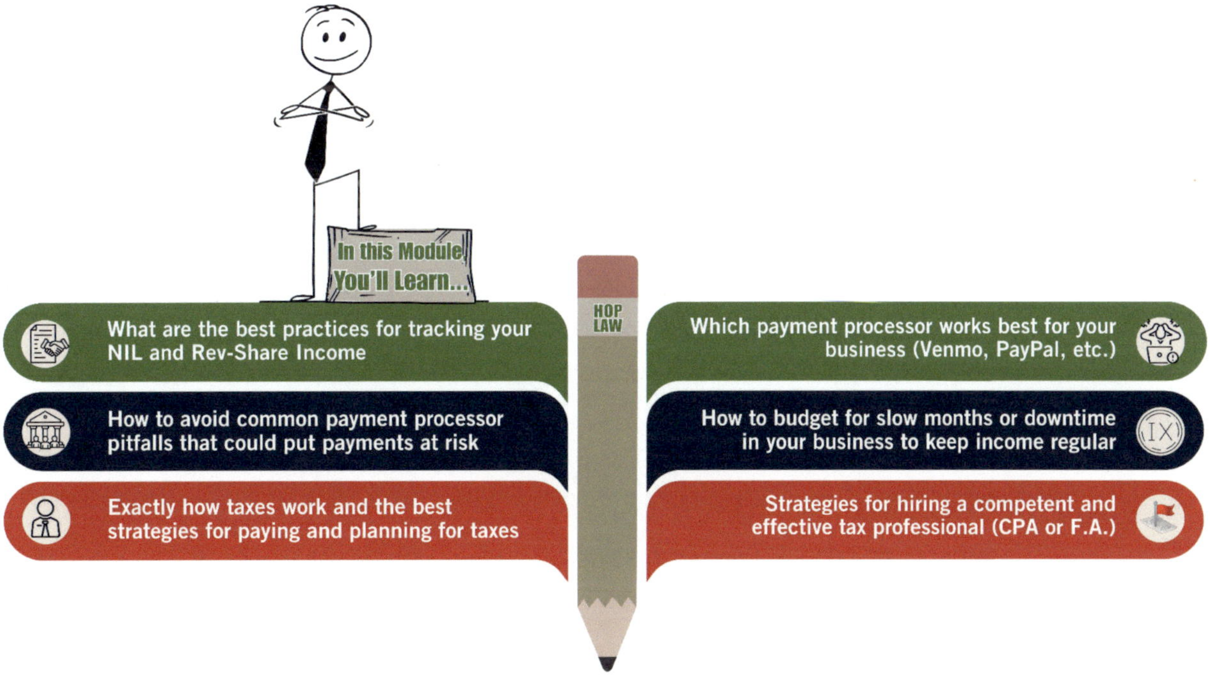

How To Track Your NIL And Rev-Share Income: Effective Methods For Diligent Recordkeeping

As a college athlete managing NIL and Rev-Share income, keeping meticulous records is essential. Thoughtful tracking not only helps you understand your cash flow but also ensures you stay compliant with tax laws, NCAA regulations, and your school's reporting requirements. Here's everything you need to know to track your income effectively.

Why Recordkeeping Matters

Financial clarity: Knowing exactly what money is coming in and when helps you budget, save, and plan.

Tax compliance: All NIL and Rev-Share payments are taxable income. Detailed records make filing taxes easier and help you avoid costly mistakes.

Eligibility protection: Transparent recordkeeping supports compliance with NCAA and school rules, protecting your eligibility and reputation.

Professionalism: Organized documents make it easier if you work with accountants, advisors, or legal professionals.

What to Track

Date of payment: When money or assets were received.

Source of income: Name and contact information of business, collective, or school paying you.

Type of income: Specify if it's an NIL endorsement, Rev-Share payment, merchandise sale, appearance fee, etc.

Payment amount and form: Cash, check, direct deposit, gifts, or barter (like free gear).

Services or deliverables provided: Social media posts, appearances made, or other obligations owed in exchange.

Invoices and contracts: Copies of signed agreements and invoices related to payments.

Tools and Methods

Spreadsheets: Simple and customizable. Build columns for all key details and update regularly.

Accounting Software: QuickBooks, Wave, or FreshBooks can automate tracking, generate reports, and help with invoicing.

Mobile Apps: Many platforms offer apps to track payments on the go.

Dedicated Business Bank Account: Used exclusively for NIL and Rev-Share income and expenses to simplify reconciliation.

Dealing with Non-Cash Income

Sometimes you may receive non-monetary compensation (e.g., free gear, travel, meal vouchers). These are taxable and should be recorded at fair market value.

Prepare for Reporting

Stay proactive about reporting your income to your school's compliance office as required. Maintain clear documentation to provide if requested.

Consistent, detailed income tracking builds the financial discipline crucial for your success both on and off the field. It keeps you compliant, prepared for taxes, and fully in control of your growing athlete business. Start simple, use tools that fit your style, and make recordkeeping a daily habit. Your future self will thank you.

Using Payment Processors (Venmo Biz, PayPal, Stripe, etc.): Benefits, Pitfalls, & Best Practices

In today's digital world, payment processors are vital tools for managing your NIL, Rev-Share, and business transactions quickly and efficiently. Platforms like Venmo Business, PayPal, and Stripe allow you to accept payments from sponsors, sell merchandise online, invoice clients, and even set up recurring payments. This section explains the benefits, common pitfalls, and best practices to leverage these tools effectively as a college athlete-entrepreneur.

Benefits of Payment Processors

Convenience and Speed: Instantly send and receive payments anytime and anywhere, simplifying cash flow management.

Multiple Payment Methods: Accept credit/debit cards, bank transfers, mobile payments, and more. Doing so allows you to offer flexibility to payers, which is standard practice.

Easy Integration: Connect smoothly with websites, e-commerce platforms, and accounting software.

Recordkeeping: Automatically track transactions and generate reports that can help with bookkeeping and tax filing.

Security: Industry-leading fraud protection and encryption help keep your money and information safe.

Global Reach: Some processors (like PayPal and Stripe) allow you to accept international payments.

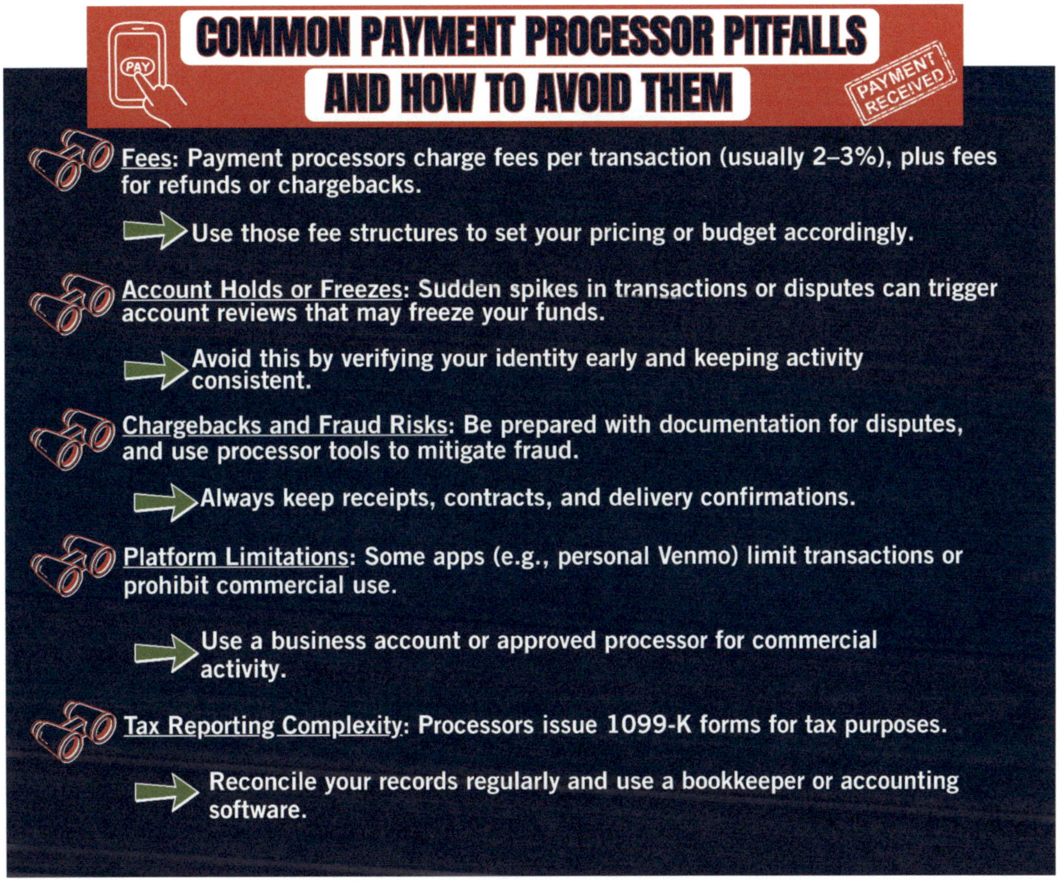

Best Practices for College Athletes Running an NIL Business

1. Choose the Right Processor for Your Needs

Venmo Business: Great for easy fan-facing transactions and simple sales; integrates with social media and is familiar to many fans. It's quick and mobile-friendly. Just make sure to upgrade to a Business Profile to stay compliant and avoid misuse of personal accounts.

PayPal: A solid all-around choice. PayPal is accepted almost everywhere, allows you to invoice brands or clients, and works well for digital products, services, or consulting. It also includes built-in buyer and seller protections, which can help reduce fraud concerns.

Stripe: Best for athletes with a full online store or who plan to offer subscriptions, digital downloads, or more complex e-commerce features. Stripe integrates smoothly with most website builders (like Shopify or Squarespace) and gives you full control over branding and customer experience.

Square: A great choice if you're doing a lot of in-person sales -- like at camps, merch tables, pop-up shops, or autograph sessions. It provides card readers, point-of-sale tools, and even inventory tracking, making it feel like a professional retail setup. Square also lets you build simple online storefronts and collect tips, which is a bonus if you're selling physical products.

Cash App for Business: Offers a low-barrier way to collect payments quickly, especially from friends, fans, or peers already using the app. It's mobile-first, fast, and easy to set up. But it's not built for long-term business growth -- it lacks strong buyer/seller protections and doesn't offer much in terms of invoicing or backend tools. It's best used for smaller transactions or temporary setups, not formal deals with brands or ongoing services.

2. Open Business Accounts

No matter which platform(s) you use, always use business profiles/accounts for transactions to separate personal and business finances and maintain professionalism.

3. Understand Fee Structures and Terms

Review fee schedules and transaction limits carefully before choosing a processor. Also look for volume discounts or bundling options if your business grows.

4. Keep Detailed Records

Download transaction history regularly and reconcile with your accounting system. Be sure to save and download digital receipts, invoices, and contracts related to transactions.

5. Communicate Clearly with Payers

Clear communication builds trust and helps you avoid missed or delayed payments. Always provide detailed instructions -- including the payment method, amount, and due date -- whether you're working with fans, brands, or sponsors. Follow up with written confirmation once payment is received, and keep records of all communication. This not only protects you in case of a dispute but also shows you're running your NIL business professionally.

6. Safeguard Your Accounts

Your payment platforms hold sensitive financial and personal information, so treat them like digital vaults. Use strong, unique passwords and enable two-factor authentication (2FA) to protect against hacking. Regularly monitor your accounts for unusual activity, such as unexpected withdrawals or login attempts. If a breach happens, it could freeze your funds, delay payments, or even lead to identity theft -- all of which can hurt your brand and business.

7. Prepare for Tax Season

Tax time is easier when you stay organized year-round. Most payment processors provide downloadable reports that summarize your income and transaction history -- use these to help your tax professional file accurately.

HOP LAW Insight: **All income counts, even if it was sent through Cash App, Venmo, PayPal, or any other payment processor. Failing to report payments can lead to penalties, audits, or delayed refunds.**

Payment processors are powerful, flexible tools that can accelerate your NIL and business activities. By choosing the right platform, understanding fees and limits, keeping thorough records, and protecting your accounts, you can manage your money professionally, avoid common pitfalls, and grow your athlete business with confidence. Harness these digital tools to simplify transactions and focus more energy on your performance and brand building.

Finding Financial Rhythm With Unpredictable NIL Business Income

As a college athlete earning NIL and Rev-Share income, your cash flow can fluctuate month to month. Some months you might land big deals or multiple payments, while others may bring little or no income. Managing this variable income with smart budgeting is essential to ensure financial stability, avoid stress, and build long-term wealth. This section offers practical strategies tailored to your unique financial landscape.

Key Budgeting Strategies

1. Track All Income and Expenses

Keep a record of every payment you receive and every purchase you make. This gives you a real view of your cash flow and financial habits. Break down income by source (NIL deals, Rev-Share, merchandise sales) so you know what's steady and what's not. Knowing which income streams are the most consistent makes planning easier month to month.

2. Separate Needs From Wants

List out your essential expenses, like savings, tuition, rent, insurance, and training equipment. Then compare those expenses to non-essentials like takeout or new clothes. Cover your must-haves first, then decide how much you can afford for extras.

3. Consider the 50/30/20 Rule (As a Guideline)

This is a simple budgeting model: 50 percent of your money goes to needs, 30 percent to wants, and 20 percent to savings and taxes. These numbers are flexible. You can shift them based on how much you earn and your current goals.

4. Build an Emergency Fund

Save a little every month with the goal of covering three to six months of basic living expenses. Having this money set aside gives you options if a deal falls through or a major cost pops up unexpectedly.

5. Set Aside Money for Taxes

Unlike a paycheck, your NIL or Rev-Share payments don't have taxes taken out. Based on your income level and location, estimate what you owe for federal, state, and self-employment taxes. Put aside approximately 20–30% of each payment in a separate savings account specifically for taxes. That way, you're ready when it's time to file.

6. Budget for Long-Term Goals

Think beyond the next few months. Whether it's saving for retirement, investing in your business, or taking extra courses, create a plan to set aside money for the future. These are the things that will help you after college, too.

7. Use Budgeting Tools

Apps like Mint, YNAB, or EveryDollar can help you track spending and stick to your budget. If you prefer spreadsheets, make sure they account for changing income and review them regularly to stay on track.

8. Plan for Irregular Expenses

Some costs don't show up every month, such as travel, off-season training, or legal fees. Instead of scrambling to pay when they come up, estimate what you'll need and build a monthly savings cushion just for those expenses.

HOP LAW Insight:

- ❖ Automate transfers to savings and tax accounts soon after income is received.
- ❖ Revisit and adjust your budget quarterly, especially during high-income seasons.
- ❖ Avoid lifestyle inflation by increasing discretionary spending only after your savings goals are met.
- ❖ Consult a financial advisor if you have large or complex cash flows.

Mastering budgeting with variable income helps you build confidence, reduce anxiety, and position yourself for success as both an athlete and an entrepreneur. A disciplined approach to money management today will pay dividends for your future, both on and off the field.

Understanding Taxes: Federal, State, Self-Employment - What You Owe & How To Prepare

As a college athlete earning money through NIL deals, Rev-Share agreements, or your own business, understanding taxes is essential. Taxes may seem complex, but knowing how federal, state, and self-employment taxes work will empower you to stay compliant, avoid surprises, and keep more of what you earn.

Most importantly, learning about the tax system -- both federal and state -- can not only save you money, but it will keep you out of legal trouble. The IRS (Internal Revenue Service) is ruthless when it comes to enforcing the U.S. Tax Code. If you fail to pay taxes, or don't pay them correctly, the IRS will likely come knocking.

The following sections are designed to give you a foundational level of understanding when it comes to how taxes work and how best to position your business when it comes to effective tax strategies. It's vital to find a trusted tax professional (ideally, a CPA) once you start a business.

Federal Income Tax Basics

The U.S. has a progressive tax system, meaning the rate you pay increases as your income increases. This is organized into tax brackets. For example, income up to a certain amount is taxed at 10%, the next portion at 12%, then 22%, and so on, up to 37% for the highest earners.

Your taxable income is your total income minus deductions (standard or itemized). The effective tax rate you pay overall is usually lower than your top bracket.

How Tax Brackets Work

Let's break down what happens if you make $100,000 in NIL money as a college athlete in 2025 (and are a single filer). Here's exactly how the federal tax would be split across brackets:

2025 Single Filer Federal Tax Brackets:

10% on $0 – $11,925

12% on $11,926 – $48,475

22% on $48,476 – $103,350

Step-by-Step Calculation:

10% Bracket:

Of that $100,000, the first $11,925 is taxed at 10% = $1,192.50

12% Bracket:

Of the remaining $88,075, the next $36,549 ($48,475 - $11,926) is taxed at 12% = $4,385.88

22% Bracket:

The remaining $51,526 of the $100,000 ($100,000 - $48,476) is taxed at 22% = $11,335.28.

Add these together for total federal tax:

Total tax owed = 1,192.50 + 4,385.88 + 11,335.28 = $16,913.66

So before accounting for any deductions, if you made $100,000, you would owe Uncle Sam $16,913.66 in federal taxes (this doesn't include state taxes). You would be in the 22% tax bracket, but you wouldn't pay 22% of your total income. Because of the tiered taxing system, you pay only a portion of the $100,000 (which was $51,526 in the above example) at the 22% rate.

We'll go over how to reduce your taxable income (called adjusted gross income) in a minute. I wanted you to get a solid understanding of how tax brackets work so that you can conceptualize the entire tax structure.

Below is the complete tax bracket for 2025:

Tax Rate	Single Filer	Married Filing Jointly	Head of Household	Married Filing Separately
10%	$0 to $11,925	$0 to $23,850	$0 to $17,000	$0 to $11,925
12%	$11,926 to $48,475	$23,851 to $96,950	$17,001 to $64,850	$11,926 to $48,475
22%	$48,476 to $103,350	$96,951 to $206,700	$64,851 to $103,350	$48,476 to $103,350
24%	$103,351 to $197,300	$206,701 to $394,600	$103,351 to $197,300	$103,351 to $197,300
32%	$197,301 to $250,525	$394,601 to $501,050	$197,301 to $250,500	$197,301 to $250,525
35%	$250,526 to $626,350	$501,051 to $751,600	$250,501 to $626,350	$250,526 to $375,800
37%	$626,351 or more	$751,601 or more	$626,351 or more	$375,801 or more

State Income Taxes

Most states tax income too, with rates varying widely. Some states like California have progressive rates up to ~13.3%, while others like Florida and Texas have no state income tax.

You'll need to file state tax returns in the state where you earn income, which might be where your school is located or where you live.

Self-Employment Tax

If you're earning money through NIL deals or Rev-Share payments, that income is typically classified as self-employment income. That means you're not considered an employee; you're running your own business, and the IRS treats you as both the worker and the employer.

Because of that, you're responsible for paying the full amount of payroll taxes (you may hear this as a FICA tax, which is Federal Insurance Contributions Act (FICA)), which includes:

- Social Security tax (12.4%)
- Medicare tax (2.9%)

Together, this is called self-employment tax, and it adds up to 15.3% of your net income. That's your income after subtracting any business expenses like gear, travel, or marketing.

Example:
If you earn $10,000 from NIL deals and spend $2,000 on business expenses, your net income is $8,000. Your self-employment tax would be:
$8,000 x 15.3% = $1,224

This tax is in addition to any federal or state income tax you may owe. That's why it's important to track expenses and set aside money regularly, so you're not caught off-guard when it's time to file.

S-Corp Election Info:

The above example shows the full amount of self-employment tax you would owe if your business did not choose the S-election discussed previously.

For illustration of how the S-Corp election could benefit you, let's say you ended up making $80,000 (after expenses) instead of the $8,000 in the above example.

Remember, if you're self-employed (without the S-election), you pay self-employment tax (that's 15.3% (Social Security + Medicare)) on 100% of your net income. That figure is reduced with the S-election. Here's how:

Scenario: No S-Election

<u>Without an S-election</u>:

- ❖ You owe self-employment tax on the full $80,000.
- ❖ That's $80,000 × 15.3% = $12,240 in self-employment tax.
- ❖ You also owe income tax on the $80,000 (based on your tax bracket).

That $12,240 is in addition to your regular income tax, not a replacement for it.

Scenario: With S-Election

Now let's say your LLC elects to be taxed as an S-Corp.

You pay yourself a reasonable salary of $42,000, which would be enough to reflect the value of the work you do, and take the remaining $38,000 as a distribution.

Here's how the taxes break down:

- ❖ You still pay income tax on the full $80,000.
- ❖ But only the $42,000 salary is subject to Social Security and Medicare taxes (15.3% = $6,426).
- ❖ The $38,000 distribution is not subject to that 15.3% tax.
- ❖ Tax savings: $12,240 – $6,426 = $5,814

That's real money you keep simply by choosing a more tax-efficient structure.

Estimated Quarterly Taxes

Unlike traditional employees, taxes are not automatically withheld from payments to your business. If you get a job at a Dave & Buster's, or some other established business, the business cuts you a paycheck (or does direct deposit). Before the business gives you what you earned, they have to take out a certain amount of money. That's called withholdings.

Withholdings include, among other taxes, the federal and state taxes you owe, along with self-employment tax (Social Security and Medicare taxes). So when you get your paycheck, Dave & Buster's have already sent a portion of your money (taxes) to the IRS and State taxing authority. At the end of the year, you add up what Dave & Buster's sent to the IRS and if they sent too much, you get a refund. If they didn't send enough, you owe the IRS the balance.

When you work for yourself, you have to estimate your tax liability for the year and pay quarterly estimated taxes to the IRS and possibly your state. Payments are generally due in April, June, September, and January.

These estimated quarterly tax payments operate like the withholdings that Dave & Buster's takes from your check and sends to the IRS. You're doing it on behalf of your business.

Deductions and Business Expenses

Deductions are expenses that reduce your taxable income. For example, if you made $100,000 in NIL deals in 2025, the IRS will want to tax you on the entire $100,000. Before they are allowed to send a tax bill to you, however, you are allowed to reduce the $100,000 figure using deductions (or what some people call "write-offs").

You can reduce taxable income by deducting legitimate expenses, such as:

- Equipment
- Travel related to appearances
- Marketing costs
- Legal and accounting fees

So, if you had $8,000 in travel expenses, paid $5,000 in legal fees, $1,000 in accounting fees, $8,000 for a car allowance, and $15,000 in business operating costs (such as paying a video editor, social media manager, etc.), then your taxable income is reduced from $100,000 to $63,000.

Using the tax bracket information above, you would go from paying $16,913.66, to $8,774.10.

HOP LAW Insight: **It's important to keep detailed records and receipts for all expenses. Some business owners claim deductions for expenses that do not qualify as a legitimate deduction just so they can reduce their tax liability. I knew a guy who worked as a welder who had a pool**

installed in his house. He claimed the in-ground pool as a business expense because he argued that he cools off the metal he welds in the pool. The IRS didn't buy it. While it's important to take advantage of every legitimate deduction, there are hefty fines and potential criminal charges for filing fraudulent tax returns.

HOP LAW Insight: It's nice to reduce your tax liability using deductions, but that also reduces your reported income. If you are applying for a loan, the bank will only want to know what your reported income is, and if you have reduced it too far (you don't make enough money to qualify for a loan), then you will hamper your chances of securing loans or other income-based programs.

Taxes are a critical part of managing your NIL and income as a self-employed college athlete. Understanding how tax brackets work, preparing for self-employment tax, staying aware of state tax obligations, and paying estimated taxes quarterly puts you in control and reduces stress. Early organization and good advice will help you make the most of your earnings while staying fully compliant.

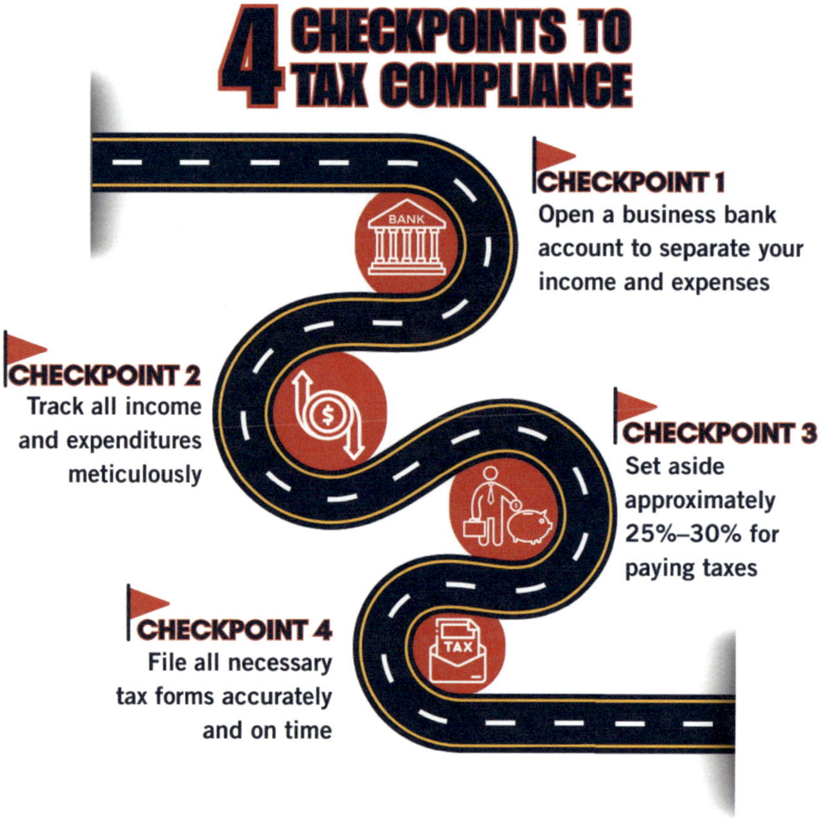

If you're ever unsure, always seek help from a trusted tax advisor and your school's compliance office to navigate the specifics of your situation.

Key Tax Forms: W-9, 1099, Estimated Quarterly Payments

The tax forms that come along with running a business can feel overwhelming at first, but once you start working with them and understand their different roles, they'll become demystified and you'll feel comfortable reading and working with them.

Also, understanding key tax forms is crucial for staying compliant with the IRS and organized. And organization is the key to success.

Here's a clear explanation of the most important forms you'll encounter, what they mean, and when you can expect to receive or file them.

Form W-9: Request for Taxpayer Identification Number and Certification
When you start working with a company or brand that will pay you, they often ask you to fill out a W-9 form.

The W-9 provides your legal name and Taxpayer Identification Number (usually your Social Security Number or EIN if you have a business).

This form does not get sent to the IRS by you; it's for the payer to use when reporting payments.

Submit a W-9 early to avoid backup withholding or payment delays.

Form 1099 (Most Common: 1099-NEC and 1099-K)
At year-end, companies or platforms that paid you $600 or more during the tax year must send you a 1099 form reporting the income they paid you. The IRS will match the company's 1099 form and what they reported paying you to what you report to the IRS the company paid you. If there is a discrepancy, it could trigger an audit.

1099-NEC: For nonemployee compensation, such as NIL endorsement payments or consulting fees.

1099-K: For payments processed via platforms like PayPal or Stripe when payment volumes and amounts meet thresholds.

You generally receive 1099s by January 31 of the following year. Keep these forms with your records because they help you accurately report your income on your tax return.

Form 1040-ES: For estimated quarterly tax payments. As discussed above, unlike employees with tax withheld from paychecks, self-employed individuals (including athletes earning NIL income) must make estimated tax payments quarterly, typically in April, June, September, and January.

Use IRS Form 1040-ES to calculate and pay federal estimated taxes. While it may feel uncomfortable paying taxes during the year, paying them on time avoids penalties and interest the IRS will charge at the end of the year if they aren't made quarterly.

Also, it feels much better to get to the tax season knowing that you don't owe the IRS anything (or, anything else, since you've been paying all along).

Schedule C (Form 1040): Used to report your business income and expenses on your personal tax return.

Schedule SE (Form 1040): Calculates your self-employment tax to be paid along with federal income tax.

Practical Tips

- Keep copies of all W-9s you submit and 1099s you receive.
- Reconcile your own income records with the 1099s to catch any discrepancies.
- Set aside money regularly throughout the year for taxes based on your income and estimated tax rates.
- Consider working with a qualified tax professional experienced with athlete income to guide you through filings and payments.

Familiarity with W-9, 1099, and estimated tax payments keeps you proactive and organized, ensuring you stay compliant and minimize year-end surprises. These forms are essential tools in your athlete-business financial toolkit, helping you confidently manage your taxes alongside your athletic career.

Hiring an Accountant: Essential Guidance for Finding Qualified Help

Managing your finances and taxes can quickly become overwhelming, especially as your NIL and business activities grow. Bringing a qualified accountant on board can be a game-changer, giving you expert guidance and peace of mind. Here's how to find the right professional and the key questions to ask before you hire.

How to Start Your Search

<u>Ask for Recommendations</u>: Talk to other athletes, coaches, compliance officers, or your school's financial aid office for trusted referrals.

<u>Look for Experience with Athlete Finances</u>: Choose someone who understands NIL, self-employment taxes, variable income, and NCAA compliance.

<u>Check Credentials</u>: Certified Public Accountants (CPA) or Enrolled Agents (EA) have formal qualifications and must abide by ethical standards.

<u>Consider Accessibility</u>: Find someone who communicates clearly and is available when you need them.

Important Questions to Ask Potential Accountants

- ❖ What experience do you have working with athletes or self-employed clients?
- ❖ How familiar are you with NIL deals, Rev-Share agreements, and related tax rules?
- ❖ What services do you provide? (Tax preparation, bookkeeping, financial planning, etc.)
- ❖ How do you charge? (Flat fees, hourly rates, package pricing)
- ❖ How do you handle estimated quarterly taxes and IRS correspondence?
- ❖ What software or tools do you use? Can you integrate with my accounting system?
- ❖ How proactive are you in helping clients with tax planning and savings?
- ❖ Can you help me understand NCAA compliance and reporting requirements?
- ❖ What is your process during tax season? How soon should I provide documents?
- ❖ How do you keep client information secure?

Working Effectively with Your Accountant

1. Keep organized records and communicate regularly.
2. Provide all income statements, expense receipts, contracts, and payment documents.
3. Ask questions if anything is unclear; your accountant should be a trusted advisor, not just a preparer.
4. Plan for periodic check-ins to adjust strategies based on your growth and changes.

Choosing the right accountant is an investment in your financial future and business success. By asking the right questions and prioritizing experience in athlete finances, you'll find a partner who helps navigate complexities, saves you money, and lets you focus on what matters most: your athletic career and personal growth.

Glossary Of Common Business And Tax Terms: Clear, Concise Definitions

Here's a review of the tax terms we've gone over so far. The longer you operate your NIL business and work the steps outlined in this book, the more of an understanding you'll have of these terms and how they fit into your business. Soon, you'll master the day-to-day and long-term operations of your business, from a tax standpoint, as well as a profit-and-loss standpoint. This glossary provides straightforward definitions of common terms you will encounter when operating your business, entering contracts, and tax filings. Learning these terms will empower your understanding of the tax world and instill confidence in your financial decisions.

Accounting Terms

Assets: Anything your business owns that has value, such as cash, equipment, or inventory.

Liabilities: Debts or obligations your business owes, like loans or unpaid bills.

Equity: The owner's share of the business, calculated as assets minus liabilities.

Revenue: The total income your business earns from sales or services before expenses.

Expenses: Costs incurred to operate your business, such as marketing, travel, or supplies.

Profit (Net Income): What's left after subtracting expenses from revenue.

Business Structure Terms

Sole Proprietorship: Simplest business form where the owner and business are legally the same.

LLC (Limited Liability Company): A legal business entity that provides liability protection for owners.

S-Corp (S Corporation): A tax status that can provide self-employment tax savings for LLCs or corporations.

EIN (Employer Identification Number): A unique number assigned by the IRS to identify your business for tax purposes.

Tax Terms

Tax Bracket: A range of income taxed at a specific rate. The U.S. tax system is progressive with multiple brackets.

Self-Employment Tax: The combined Social Security and Medicare taxes paid by self-employed individuals (about 15.3%).

W-9 Form: A request for your taxpayer ID number and certification, usually sent to companies that pay you.

1099 Form: A form reporting income paid to you by businesses or payment platforms.

Schedule C: Tax form used to report income and expenses from your business.

Estimated Taxes: Quarterly payments you make to cover income and self-employment taxes.

Financial Management Terms

Budget: A plan that estimates income and expenses over a period.

Cash Flow: Movement of money in and out of your business.

Recordkeeping: The process of organizing and storing financial documents systematically.

Invoice: A bill you send to customers or sponsors detailing the amount owed and payment terms.

Banking and Payment Terms

Business Bank Account: A separate bank account for your business finances.

Payment Processor: Services like PayPal, Venmo Business, or Stripe that handle electronic transactions.

Merchant Account: A bank account that allows businesses to accept credit or debit card payments.

Keep this glossary handy as you manage your athlete business. Knowing these terms helps you communicate clearly with professionals, understand contracts, and make informed financial decisions.

MODULE EIGHT

DOLLARS & SENSE: BUILDING WEALTH WITH SMART MONEY MOVES

Building long-term wealth doesn't wait until after your playing days; it works best when you begin early. Even modest contributions from NIL, Rev-Share, or your business income can compound over decades into millions of dollars. Time is your greatest advantage in investing, and the sooner you begin, the more powerful the compounding effect becomes. But starting early is the key.

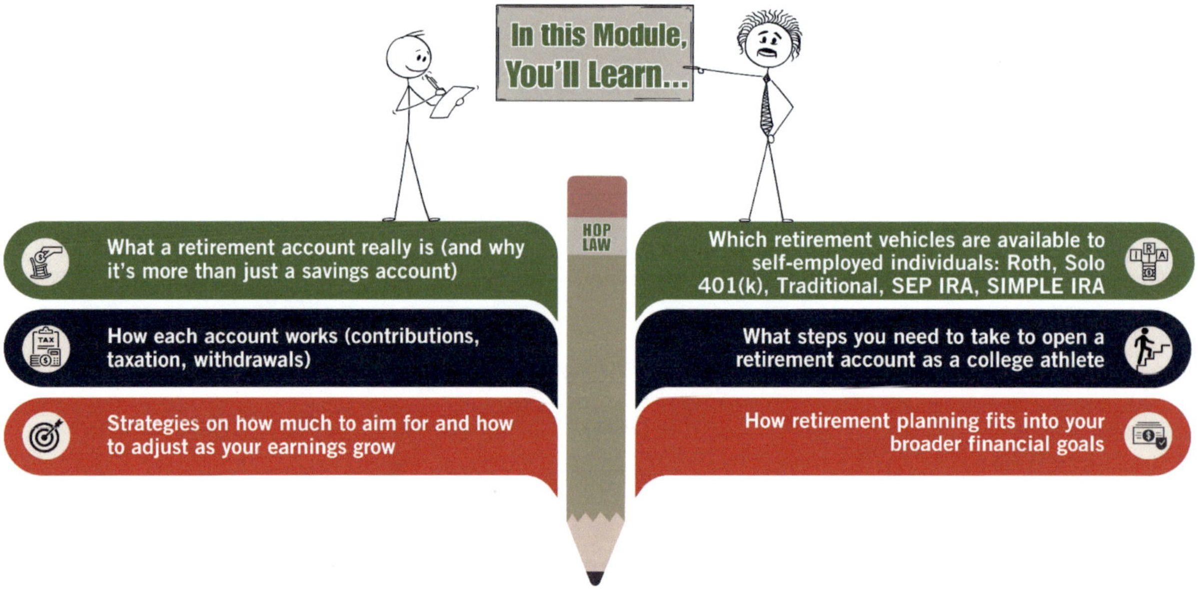

By the time you finish Module Eight, you'll understand not just *why* retirement accounts are crucial, but also *which* ones make sense for your career right now and most importantly, *how* to take action.

Why You Should Open a Retirement Account Now

We'll get into specifics in a page or two, but for now, just know that opening a retirement account is the first step to creating financial freedom, not just for you, but for future generations in your family. With steady discipline and the power of compounding interest, you're uniquely positioned to hit your first million by 50. That might not sound young now, but at 50 -- about twenty years into a job -- realizing you may need another 15 years to retire (if you're lucky), the regret of not saving will land hard. The financial decisions you make now (if they're smart) will give you the power to choose, which negates regret. And if done correctly, you'll be able to leave a solid financial foundation for your children and their children.

At a glance, here's a few benefits to opening that first retirement account:

Tax-advantaged growth: Your contributions grow either tax-deferred or tax-free, allowing compounding to build on itself without annual taxation dragging performance.

Early independence: Starting now gives you a head start toward financial goals -- home ownership, business investment, or retiring (or semi-retiring) early.

Edge over late starters: Most people delay investing until their 30s or 40s; by then, much of the "easy growth" is already lost.

Peace of mind: With a retirement fund underway, riskier business ventures feel safer, because you've already built a foundation.

Understanding The Different Types Of Retirement Accounts & How They Work

1. Roth IRA (Individual Retirement Account)

Think of the Roth as your "taxes now, freedom later" bucket. It's especially useful early in your career when your tax rate is likely lower than it will be down the road. You get flexibility, too: contributions (not the growth) can be pulled out any time if "life" happens. If your income climbs and phases you out later, you'll be glad you started while eligible. Fund it consistently, invest in broad, low-cost index funds, and let compounding do the heavy lifting.

Contributions: You put in money you've already paid taxes on (post-tax). For 2025, you can contribute up to $7,000 per year (or $8,000 if age 50+), subject to income limits.

Growth: Your investments (stocks, bonds, mutual funds) grow tax-free.

Withdrawals: Qualified withdrawals in retirement (after age 59½) are completely tax-free -- including investment gains. You can withdraw your contributions (but not gains) any time without taxes or penalties.

Great for: Investing your NIL generated income (or any income) adjusting your tax burden when you retire and start to take withdrawals (because these withdrawals will be tax-free).

2. Traditional IRA

This is your "lower my tax bill today" option. It can make sense in a high-income year or when a deduction pushes you into a better bracket or unlocks credits. Just remember you're deferring taxes, not dodging them -- you'll pay ordinary income tax on withdrawals later (compared to the Roth withdrawals that are tax-free). If you expect a lower tax rate in retirement, the trade can be worth it. Pair with Roth in different years to diversify your future tax picture.

Contributions: Made with pre- or post-tax dollars (depending on your situation). Contributions may be tax-deductible -- good if you want an upfront break. The annual limit is the same as for Roth IRA.

Growth: Investments grow tax-deferred.

Withdrawals: Taxed as income at retirement.

Great for: Those who want a tax break up front, or anticipate being in a lower tax bracket in retirement.

3. SEP IRA (Simplified Employee Pension IRA)

Great when your business income spikes and you want a simple, high-limit way to stash pre-tax dollars fast. Setup is quick, admin is light, and you can wait until tax time to decide how much to contribute -- handy when income is lumpy. The catch: if you have employees, you generally must contribute for them, too, using the same percentage. If you're solo and want "easy and big," a SEP fits.

Designed For: Self-employed individuals or small business owners (like athletes running their own NIL business).

Contributions: Made by the business, not as personal contributions. You can contribute up to 25% of your net earnings from self-employment (up to $70,000 for 2025), which is far higher than the personal IRA limit.

Growth: Tax-deferred until withdrawal at retirement.

Withdrawals: Taxed as ordinary income after age 59½.

Great for: Athletes who have high annual NIL/business income and want to save more on a pre-tax basis.

4. Solo 401(k) (a.k.a. Individual 401(k))

This is the power tool for one-person businesses. You can combine an employee piece with an employer piece, which often lets you save more at lower income levels than a SEP. You also get Roth flexibility inside the plan, and the option to borrow via a plan loan if allowed. The tradeoff is a bit more paperwork and earlier setup deadlines. If you're serious about maximizing contributions and controlling taxes, it's worth the structure.

Designed For: Self-employed individuals with no W-2 employees other than a spouse (perfect for athlete-run businesses).

Contributions: You contribute in two roles, as employee and as employer.

> Employee deferral: Up to $23,500 for 2025 (plus $7,500 catch-up if 50+), pre-tax or Roth.
>
> Employer profit-share: Up to 25% of net self-employment income (sole prop/LLC) or compensation (S-Corp/W-2).

Combined cap: Up to $70,000 for 2025 (or more if 50+), across deferral + profit-share.

Growth: Tax-deferred (pre-tax) or tax-free on qualified withdrawals (Roth sub-account).

Withdrawals: Pre-tax amounts taxed as ordinary income in retirement; Roth qualified withdrawals tax-free. Early withdrawals may incur penalties.

Great for: Athletes with strong business income who want higher limits than IRAs, Roth flexibility, and the ability to contribute both as "employee" and "employer."

5. SIMPLE IRA (Savings Incentive Match Plan for Employees)

Pick this when you want a legit retirement plan for you (and any staff) without turning your life into HR. It's easy to open, payroll-friendly, and forces helpful discipline through required employer contributions. Downsides: lower limits than a 401(k) and a steep penalty if you withdraw in the first two years. If you're running a lean operation and value "set it up, keep it moving," SIMPLE does the job.

Designed For: Small businesses with ≤100 employees that don't sponsor another plan; easy way to cover yourself and any staff.

Contributions:

> Employee deferral: Up to $16,500 for 2025 (plus $3,500 catch-up if 50+).
>
> Employer contribution (required): Either match up to 3% of compensation or a 2% nonelective contribution for all eligible employees.

Growth: Tax-deferred until withdrawal.

Withdrawals: Taxed as ordinary income in retirement. Early withdrawals generally face a 10% penalty; 25% penalty if taken within the first two years of participation.

Great for: Athletes running a small operation who want simple setup and required employer contributions, but don't need the higher limits and admin of a 401(k).

Here's a breakdown of key retirement account options relevant for self-employed or NIL-earning athletes. Use this as a reference when deciding what fits your situation.

Account Type	Contribution Source	Tax Treatment	Withdrawals / Penalties	Who It Benefits
Roth IRA	After-tax (post-tax dollars)	Growth is **tax-free**	Qualified withdrawals after 59½ are tax-free; contributions (your principal) can often be withdrawn tax-free early	Athletes expecting higher income later; want tax flexibility
Traditional IRA	Pre-tax (or deductible) in some cases	Growth is tax-deferred	Withdrawals taxed as ordinary income in retirement; early withdrawal penalties may apply	Those wanting upfront tax deduction and expecting lower rates later
SEP IRA	Employer (your business) contributes	Contributions are pre-tax	Withdrawals taxed as income	High-earning years; want to funnel more money into retirement than IRAs allow
Solo 401(k) / Individual 401(k)	You as employee + business as "employer"	You contribute up to limit (pre-tax or Roth optional), business matches	Withdrawals taxed unless Roth, early withdrawal penalties apply	Entrepreneurs with high NIL/business earnings; want more contribution flexibility
SIMPLE IRA	Employer matching contributions	Pre-tax contributions	Withdrawals taxed as income	Those with modest earnings who want something simpler than 401(k)

How To Open A Retirement Account Step-By-Step

1. Choose an Account Type

Compare the benefits of Roth, Traditional, and SEP IRAs. Many young athletes start with a Roth IRA for its flexibility, but if you're earning significant business income, consider a SEP IRA too.

2. Pick a Brokerage or Bank

Leading online brokerages include Fidelity, Vanguard, Charles Schwab, TD Ameritrade, and others. Most offer user-friendly apps and commission-free trades.

Some banks also offer IRAs but may have fewer investment choices.

3. Gather Required Information

- Social Security Number
- Personal information (address, phone, etc.)
- Employment and income details (for SEP IRA, business documentation may be needed)
- Bank account info for transferring funds

4. Complete the Application Online or In Person

Applications are usually simple and take less than 30 minutes online.

For a SEP IRA, you may need to fill out IRS Form 5305-SEP; most brokerages guide you through this.

5. Fund the Account

Start with an initial contribution or set up automatic transfers from your bank account.

You can contribute in a lump sum or over time, as long as you don't exceed annual limits.

6. Choose Your Investments

IRAs let you choose how to invest: mutual funds, index funds, stocks, bonds, and more.

If unsure where to start, many brokerages offer target-date funds based on your age and estimated retirement year.

Important Tips for Maximizing NIL & Rev-Share Money

- Start early -- even small amounts, deposited on a routine basis, add up!
- Make sure your NIL/business income is reported as earned income for IRA eligibility.
- If you may need money in the next few years, avoid investing everything into IRAs -- IRAs are designed for long-term savings. You can use high-yield savings accounts to invest at a lower (but still solid) rate, while still having access to the money.
- Review and adjust your investments annually as your career evolves.
- Seek guidance from a financial advisor if you have large or irregular income.

Opening a retirement account is a powerful way to set yourself up for lifelong financial health. By starting now, you'll harness the benefits of early investment, tax-advantaged growth, and the discipline to secure your future on and off the field.

Learning The Key Investment Fundamentals

Building wealth isn't just about how much money you earn -- it's about the money you make, making money. And the way the money makes money is through smart investing. Understanding how investments grow over time is essential for college athletes who want financial success beyond their athletic careers. Here's a complete, practical overview of key investment types, how they work, and why starting early makes a powerful difference.

Compound Interest

The first aspect of investing and building wealth is understanding how compound interest works, and works well in your favor. Compound interest is the quiet engine that grows money in the background. You earn a return on what you put in, and then your returns start earning their own returns. That second part is the difference-maker: when money starts making money.

Instead of the money you put into a retirement account growing in a straight line, it starts to curve upward because each month the base gets a little bigger. A simple way to estimate the effect is the "Rule of 72": divide 72 by your yearly growth rate to see roughly how many years it takes to double. At 8% growth (your money making 8%), money doubles about every nine years. Put in $1,000, let it sit, and time does more work than you do.

Why start now? Because compounding needs time to show its power. Starting at 20 instead of 30 can mean you end up with two or three times as much, even if you invest the same amount each month. That's not because you picked a special fund or chased big risks; it's because you gave your money more "cycles" to grow and re-grow. The practical move is simple: automate a small, steady contribution, leave it alone, and let compound interest do what it does. Waiting costs you the one ingredient you can't replace later -- time.

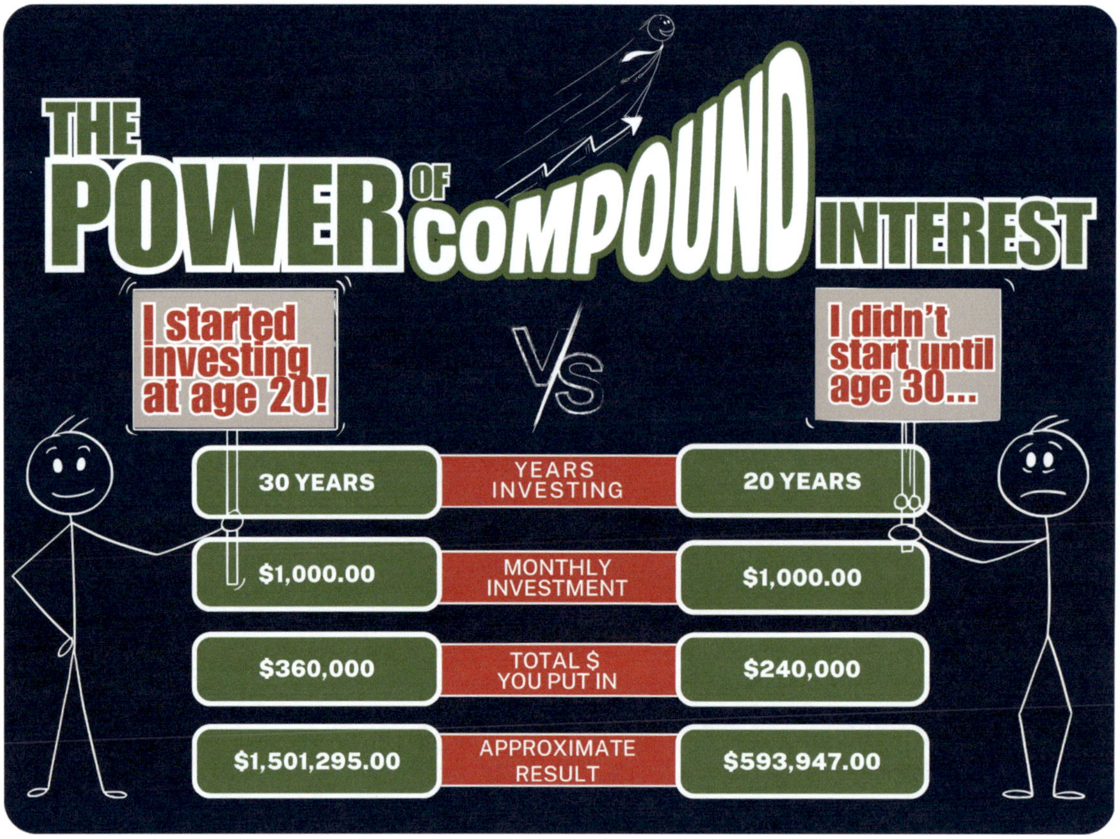

Main Investment Options

1. Stocks

What Stocks Are: Owning stock in a company means that you have an ownership interest in the company that you have stock in. Shares are different from stocks. Shares are the individual units or pieces of the company that you hold stock in. So, it would be where you buy a certain number of shares of a company's stock. Once you buy those shares, you become a shareholder of the company.

How You Earn Money: Companies sell stocks to raise money to grow, and as a shareholder, you can make money if the company does well and its stock price increases.

You can also earn dividends, which are a portion of the company's profits, or lose money if the stock price falls.

Risk: Stocks generally have high returns over long periods, but prices can fluctuate in the short term, which makes the risk high if you do daytrading rather than are in it for the long haul. You can minimize the risk associated with buying stocks by owning stocks from different companies and industries, called diversifying.

2. Index Funds

What Index Funds Are: While you can buy stock in one company and track the company's profitability, hoping to buy low and sell high, for a quick return, an index fund is a group of those stocks you buy at one time. Think of an index fund as a portfolio of stocks from hundreds of companies. You can't research each one of those companies and buy a small amount of shares for each one, so you rely on pre-built index funds to do that research for you. Investment companies also manage those funds, where they continue to track the companies' performances and edit the fund to try to make it as profitable as possible.

How You Earn Money: Generally, an index fund tracks a specific market, such as the S&P 500. Because it tracks a specific market, and those markets generally have a steady return on your investment (approximately 8%), they are an effective, low-cost way to build wealth over time (rather than trying your hand at daytrading). This method is called "passive investing" because you are just tracking the market, not trying to beat it, and you get to take advantage of **compound interest.** The key is to continue to buy into the index fund of your choice, even when the market takes a hit here and there. When you buy shares when the market is low, you are buying at a reduced cost.

Similar to stocks, as the value of the overall market or sector rises, so does your index fund. And just like stocks, index funds can also pay dividends.

Risk: Investing in index funds carries very little risk. Index funds are much less riskier than picking individual stocks and hoping for a payout. The index fund also charges smaller or no fees, while daytrading can cost with each transaction. Index funds are great for those investors who are just starting out and are ready to invest long term for steady growth.

3. High Yield Savings Accounts

What High-Yield Savings Accounts (HYSA) Are: A HYSA is a bank or credit union savings account that pays a higher interest rate than a regular savings account. Most are offered by online banks (lower overhead = better rates). Your money stays in cash -- no stocks or bonds -- so the balance won't swing with the market. As long as the bank is FDIC-insured (or NCUA for credit unions), your deposits are protected up to the legal limits, which makes this one of the safest places to park short-term cash.

How You Earn Money: Banks pay you interest (quoted as APY -- annual percentage yield) that compounds over time. The APY is variable and can move up or down with the interest-rate environment. You don't need to "pick" anything like you do with stocks or index funds -- just deposit and let the interest accrue. Because the account is liquid, you can transfer money out to a checking account or spend it when needed. Many HYSAs have no monthly fees and no minimums, so every dollar you keep there is actually working for you.

Risk: There's no market risk, but there is opportunity cost and inflation risk. HYSAs generally earn less than long-term investments like stock index funds (4-5%), so they're not a growth vehicle for decades-long goals. Rates can drop, and inflation can outpace your APY in some years. Use HYSAs for your emergency fund (3–6 months of expenses), near-term goals (0–24 months), or money you can't afford to lose. For best results, choose an FDIC/NCUA-insured bank, confirm there are no monthly fees, and automate transfers so you consistently build the cushion without thinking about it.

4. Real Estate

What Real Estate Investing Is: Buying property -- single-family homes, condos, small multifamily, or commercial space -- with the goal of building equity and generating income. You can own directly (you hold the deed), partner with others, or buy shares of real estate through REITs (real estate investment trusts) if you want exposure without being a landlord. Real estate is real; it's tangible, usually local, and heavily shaped by financing costs (how much it costs you to get into it) and neighborhood dynamics, so due diligence matters more than hype. You have to be a student of the financial and housing markets to be successful. That means knowing how much money costs (for financing purposes) and knowing the cities, neighborhoods, and streets you're looking to buy a house in and on.

How You Earn Money: Two main engines -- cash flow and appreciation. Cash flow is the rent left over after mortgage, taxes, insurance, HOA, maintenance, and reserves. Appreciation is the property's value rising over time. Real estate also offers tax tools like depreciation (which can shelter some rental income), expense write-offs (deductions), and -- if you sell and reinvest properly -- 1031 exchanges to defer capital gains. Leverage (using a mortgage) can amplify returns because you control a large asset with a smaller down payment, but it cuts both ways if rents or values drop. You can also choose to buy and flip houses. The ones who know how to do major repairs on broken down houses are the ones who are profitable with flipping houses.

Risk: Real estate is not hands-off, by any means. If you are hands-off with your real estate business, then you're likely going to fail. Vacancies, repairs, surprise assessments, changing local laws, and interest-rate swings can turn a "great deal" into a headache. Property is illiquid -- you can't sell a bathroom to raise cash -- and transaction costs are high. Run conservative numbers: model realistic rents, a vacancy factor (5–10%), repair and maintenance reserves (e.g., 10% of rent), and stress-test your mortgage at higher rates.

Bringing in professional management is the safest path to a truly hands-off operation. Property management companies typically take a percentage of the gross rent (e.g., 15%) but take care of all repairs and maintenance (they hire the professionals to do the work and send you the bill). Using PMCs makes running the business easier, but much less profitable.

If you want simpler exposure, consider publicly traded REITs for diversification and liquidity, knowing market prices will still move. For direct ownership, build a cash cushion, know landlord-tenant rules, and insure properly (landlord policy, liability, maybe umbrella).

Smart Investment Tips for Starting Out

- Start early: The sooner you invest, the stronger the compounding effect.
- Diversify: Don't put all your money in one type or one investment. Stocks, funds, and real estate work well together.
- Stay consistent: Make regular monthly or yearly contributions, even if small.
- Invest for the long term: Avoid chasing quick wins; let time and compounding work for you.
- Learn before diving in: Research, use simulation apps, or consider talking to a financial advisor.

Investing, and investing early, is the key to building wealth that lasts. By understanding and using stocks, index funds, HYSAs, and real estate -- and harnessing the magic of compound interest -- you'll give yourself the best chance for financial freedom, security, and opportunity no matter where your athletic career leads.

How NIL Deals & Rev-Share Contracts Affect FAFSA & Scholarships

Understanding how earnings from NIL deals and Rev-Share contracts affect your financial aid is essential for every college athlete. These new sources of income can change your FAFSA (Free Application for Federal Student Aid) status and influence scholarship eligibility, so it's important to know what to expect and how to plan ahead.

FAFSA: How NIL and Rev-Share Money Is Counted

NIL and Rev-Share income are treated as taxable income -- just like a part-time job, gigs, or self-employment earnings.

When filling out your FAFSA, you'll report your prior year's income tax information. The amount of money you made from NIL, endorsements, or Rev-Share agreements should be included where it asks about "student income."

Earnings can reduce your financial aid eligibility. Higher income may raise your Expected Family Contribution (EFC -- soon called "Student Aid Index" (SAI)) and decrease need-based aid for the following academic year. A higher total income, including your earnings, generally leads to a high EFC/SAI because it suggests a greater ability to contribute to educational costs.

There is a "student income protection allowance" that enables students to earn up to a certain amount ($11,770 for the 2025-2026 school year) before it affects federal aid. Amounts earned above this threshold will increase your EFC/SAI and can reduce federal grants and subsidized loans.

NIL income must also be reported as self-employment income on your tax return, and FAFSA will account for this accordingly.

Scholarships: What You Need to Know

Athletic scholarships are usually not affected by outside income -- but some schools, conferences, or sports may have specific rules.

Need-based scholarships and grants: Any increased income, including from NIL or Rev-Share deals, can impact eligibility if your financial need decreases on paper.

Private or third-party scholarships: Each may have its own rules about outside income, so always check their guidelines and communicate with scholarship administrators.

Special cases: Some campus or state scholarships require disclosure of new income streams and could adjust awards if they find significant changes.

Rev-Share Contracts and Financial Aid

Rev-Share income (from athletic departments, collectives, or group licensing) functions like other NIL earnings for FAFSA and scholarship purposes -- it's taxable, reportable income that counts when calculating aid.

If you receive Rev-Share payments through a collective or university, confirm if those funds are considered student income or financial aid on school records.

Always keep clear records of all payments, contracts, and how funds are delivered for accurate FAFSA and scholarship reporting.

Action Steps and Tips

Keep organized records of all NIL and Rev-Share income, contracts, and related expenses.

When completing your FAFSA, be honest and thorough in reporting earned income.

If you're unsure, consult your financial aid office or campus compliance office; they can clarify how specific contracts will affect your aid.

Remember to update FAFSA and scholarship offices promptly if you anticipate major changes in your income status that might affect your aid for next year.

NIL and Rev-Share income provides amazing opportunities, but it often comes with new financial aid responsibilities. Stay informed, keep excellent records, and seek advice early -- so your business success doesn't come at the expense of your college funding.

Setting Up Health Insurance & Disability Protection

Navigating health insurance and disability coverage is vital for college athletes managing their finances and future. Medical emergencies or unexpected injuries can have major consequences -- both for your athletic career and your financial wellbeing. This section covers what every student-athlete should know about securing robust health and disability protection.

Health Insurance: Basics and Options

School-Provided Insurance: Many colleges offer limited health insurance for students. There is a health care facility on campus and they see students for most illnesses and injuries. The cost of the health care is built into your tuition, and the cost of medications is low (e.g., $1 or $2 for most medications). For athletes, health insurance is likely required, and the plans may cover sports injuries, basic doctor visits, and preventive care, but often have exclusions, limited networks, or caps on certain costs.

Parent/Guardian Plans: You may remain on a family policy until age 26 under federal law. Confirm your eligibility and what's covered while away at college.

Marketplace Plans: If you're not covered through school or a parent, you can buy individual health insurance via the Affordable Care Act marketplace or directly from health insurers. These plans can cover more services, but premiums vary with deductibles and benefits.

Medicaid: If your income is low, you may qualify for state Medicaid programs offering comprehensive coverage at little or no cost.

Key Health Insurance Factors:

- Network: Make sure local hospitals and doctors accept your plan.
- Deductible/Out-of-Pocket: Calculate what you'll pay before insurance kicks in and your share of costs for care.
- Prescription Coverage: Athletes often need medications for performance or recovery -- double-check prescriptions are covered.
- Sports Injury Coverage: Confirm your plan covers athletic injuries, especially if you compete in higher-risk sports or outside official college events.

Disability Protection: Why It Matters

Disability insurance pays you a benefit if injury or illness prevents you from earning NIL, Rev-Share, or other income. This coverage is often overlooked, but can be crucial -- especially for those whose business or athletic earnings depend on their health.

Short-Term Disability Insurance: Pays a portion of your lost income (usually 40–60%) for a limited time after short-term injury or illness.

Long-Term Disability Insurance: Provides longer-term coverage if an injury keeps you from working or competing for months or years.

Securing health insurance and disability protection isn't just about meeting requirements -- it's about safeguarding your income, career goals, and peace of mind. Take the time to review your options, fill gaps in coverage, and build a safety net that supports you both in the game and in your business endeavors.

MODULE NINE

BUILDING & PROTECTING YOUR BRAND & INTELLECTUAL PROPERTY

Picture this: You're walking on campus and see your name and picture on someone's T-shirt and you know you didn't approve the design or use. Or, you try to get your name as your instagram handle but you see that a fan account has already grabbed your handle before you do. Even worse, you get a "brand deal" where the company wants rights to your logo forever for a one-time check. None of this is hypothetical -- it's the everyday internet. This module slows things down and hands you the controls: how to decide what your brand stands for, name it well, lock it down with the right protections, and build a clean, professional presence that attracts the right partners. You'll learn how to turn your personal story into real assets -- registered, licensable, and trackable -- so opportunities don't just find you; they fit you.

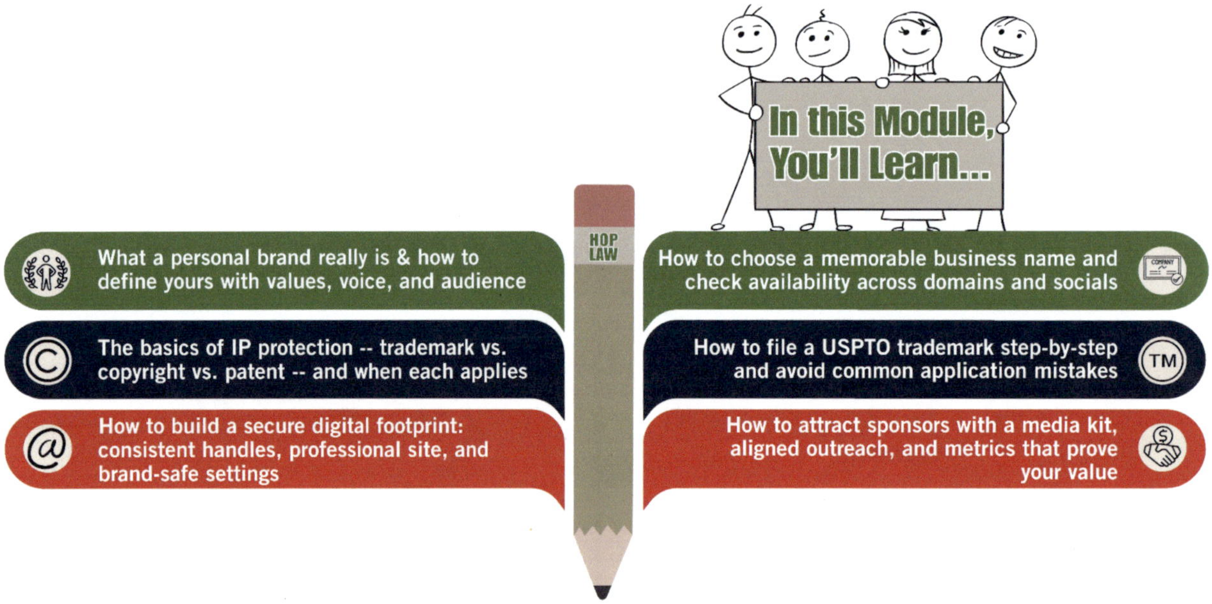

The Elements & Importance Of Your Personal Brand

A personal brand is how you present yourself to the world -- your unique personality, values, skills, and reputation combined into a memorable image that people recognize and connect with. It's not just a logo or social media handle; it's the story you tell and the experience others have when they interact with you.

Your personal brand answers questions like: Who am I? What do I stand for? Why should sponsors, fans, or partners care about and invest in me? It shapes how you're perceived both on and off the field.

Why Branding is Essential for College Athletes

For college athletes, personal branding is more important than ever because of the rise of NIL opportunities. Your brand can open doors to endorsement deals, merchandise sales, speaking engagements, and partnerships, among many other opportunities. It's the difference between being a name on a roster and being someone a company can confidently invest in. When a brand, collective, or local business looks at you, they're not just looking at stats -- they're looking for a clear story, a defined audience, and proof you can move people to pay attention.

Building a strong personal brand helps you in the following areas:

Attract Sponsorships and Endorsements: Brands want to partner with athletes who align with their values and have an engaged audience. That means they're scanning for signals: clean visuals, a clear message, consistent engagement, and basic professionalism (media kit, contact info, past collaborations). When you can show audience demographics, engagement rates, and examples of posts that performed, you make it easy for a sponsor to say yes and justify a real budget.

Differentiate Yourself: In competitive sports and business, standing out with a unique brand gives you an edge. Maybe you're the STEM major who breaks down recovery tech, the community-first leader who hosts youth clinics, or the creator who makes simple "day-in-the-life" content that actually helps younger athletes. Clear positioning helps people remember you, and being memorable is what gets you called first when a campaign needs a face.

Control Your Narrative: Shaping your own story helps avoid misunderstandings and builds trust with fans. If you don't tell your story, someone else will -- and they'll get the details wrong. A defined brand gives reporters, partners, and new followers the right "quick take" on who you are and what you do. That saves you time, prevents confusion, and turns interviews, features, and appearances into opportunities instead of risks.

Create Lasting Opportunities: A good brand can sustain you even after your athletic career ends. Deals may start with gear or a small stipend, but a real brand translates into paid appearances, signature products, licensing, and doors into media, entrepreneurship, or coaching. Alumni networks, local businesses, and national sponsors all prefer working with someone who knows how to present themselves, deliver on commitments, and communicate value. That carries forward long after the last game -- into jobs, ventures, and partnerships you can build on for years.

A defined brand is a business asset. It helps you price your value, negotiate better terms, document results, and line up the next opportunity before the current one ends. If you're going to do the work on the field, you might as well make sure the market can recognize and reward it.

Examples of Successful Athlete Brands

Many top athletes serve as great examples of personal branding:

Caitlin Clark (Iowa, WBB)
Clear story (long-range shooting + calm under pressure), massive engagement, and hardworking, family-friendly image. She translated performance into national sponsors and consistent messaging, which made it easy for brands to justify real budgets (attracts sponsors, differentiates, creates post-college runway).

Angel Reese (LSU, WBB)
Distinctive persona ("Bayou Barbie"), fashion/beauty crossover, but also gives off hardworking, unapologetic confidence. She leans into style + performance, controls her narrative in interviews and social media, and opens doors beyond sports (fashion, lifestyle) -- that's differentiation and long-tail opportunity.

Olivia "Livvy" Dunne (LSU, Gymnastics)
Elite creator discipline (high-quality, on-brand content at scale), lifestyle alignment, and a relentlessly professional presentation. She shows audience data and produces sponsor-ready content calendars -- brands see reliability, reach, and fit (attracts sponsors, controls narrative, durable post-college platform).

Suni Lee (Auburn, Gymnastics)
Olympic champion who reframed her story for the college stage: humility, excellence, and resilience. She aligns with health/fitness/empowerment verticals, keeps messaging tight, and leverages community appearances -- trusted, values-aligned partnerships (differentiates, attracts sponsors, extends opportunities).

Haley & Hanna Cavinder (Miami, WBB)
A polished, business-first approach: media kits, consistent twin brand, fitness/lifestyle positioning, and disciplined posting. They convert engagement into repeat partnerships and spin up their own ventures -- proof of a brand that functions like a company (attracts sponsors, controls narrative, long-term opportunity).

Shedeur Sanders (Jackson State/Colorado, FB)
Performance meets production: behind-the-scenes content, QB leadership angle, and a distinct personal style. He packages his story (work, preparation, family expectations) into sponsor-ready narratives and consistent visuals -- easy for brands to plug into (differentiates, controls narrative, post-college upside).

While these athletes are well-branded and recognized stars, building your personal brand starts small -- with authenticity and consistency. They all started small and grew their brands into large, durable platforms by repeating simple habits: share something real, keep promises, and choose opportunities that match their values. Your version of that might be a weekly post that actually helps your audience, a clean website, or one thoughtful partnership you can deliver on. Do that long enough and your reputation compounds -- quietly at first, then all at once.

Key Things College Athletes Should Know

Your brand is created by both you and others. What you post, how you show up, and how people talk about you all add up. If you don't define the story, someone else will -- so be intentional and consistent about what you put into the world.

Consistency is key. Keep the same tone, visuals, and message across social, interviews, community events, and deals. Repetition builds recognition; mixed signals confuse fans and sponsors and make partnerships harder to close.

Authenticity matters. Choose opportunities that fit your real values and interests. Audiences can tell when something is forced, and forced content weakens trust and future earning potential.

Your brand evolves. You'll grow, and your focus may change. Update your positioning on purpose -- explain the shift, clean up old assets when needed, and keep a simple through-line so people can follow along.

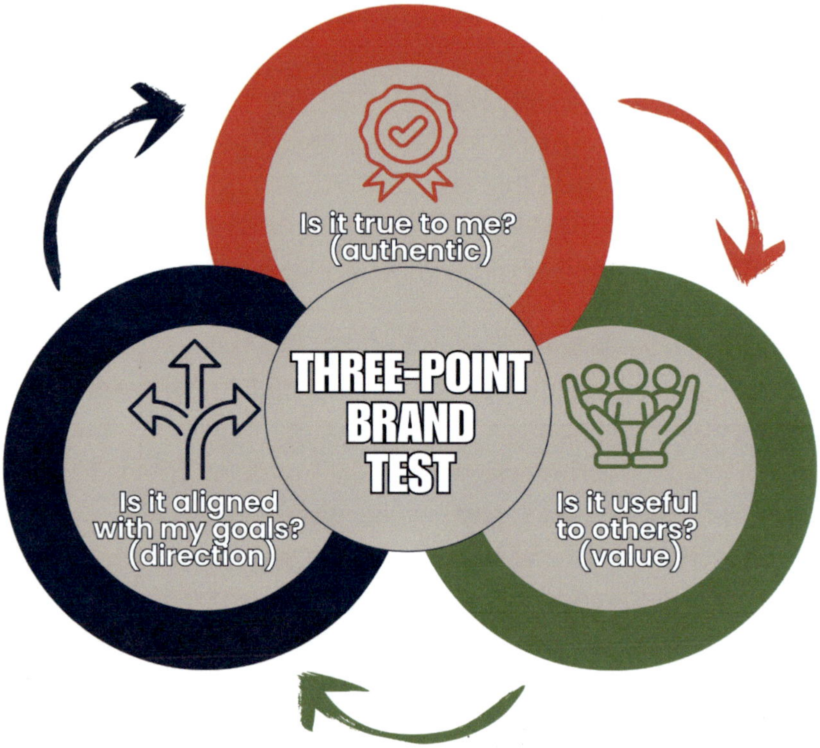

Personal branding is a powerful tool in your athletic journey. Even if you're not actively pursuing NIL deals, as an athlete, you have a brand from a pure athletic standpoint. Coaches know your personality as a player, tendencies on the field or court, and reputation before they even recruit you. The same goes for brands when they are choosing to work with you. When it comes to your brand as a business, starting with a clear understanding helps you intentionally build a brand that represents you and supports your goals on and off the field.

Defining & Crafting Your Brand's Vision, Personality, & Values

Your brand personality is the set of human traits and emotions that you want others to associate with you. It could be confident, authentic, inspiring, approachable, or any blend that feels true to who you are. Alongside personality, your core values -- such as integrity, perseverance, or community -- form the foundation of your brand and guide your decisions and behavior. Those aspects of your brand come together through the vision you have for your brand. Above all else, authenticity should form the foundation of your brand; people will be able to tell if you are being fake or real when it comes to how you present yourself in public.

To synthesize your brand's vision, personality, and values, ask yourself:

- ❖ What qualities do I want to be known for?
- ❖ What values are non-negotiable in my athletic and business life?

By defining these early and clearly, you create a consistent, relatable, and trustworthy image that resonates with others.

To build on that, translate your answers into a simple "brand filter" you can use before you post, partner, or speak. A brand filter is one sentence and three bullets. Sentence: "I want to be known for ______." Bullets: (1) The values I won't compromise are ______; (2) My audience should feel ______ after interacting with me; (3) I say yes to opportunities that fit ______ and no to those that don't.

Next, pick 3–5 "content pillars" that match your personality and values (for example: training habits, community work, style/fashion, academics, or entrepreneur life). These pillars keep your message focused so partners and fans know what you stand for, and they help you avoid chasing random trends that don't fit.

Create a short brand voice guide: a few words for tone (e.g., direct, encouraging, calm), a list of phrases you use, and phrases you avoid. Add a basic visual kit -- colors, type, and two or three rules for photos (e.g., bright natural light, clean backgrounds). Personality isn't just what you say; it's how your presence looks and feels.

Define your "brand promise" in one line: what someone can reliably expect from you. Then add two proof points -- real things you do that back it up (e.g., weekly clinic videos, consistent community appearances, transparent updates on goals). Promises without proof reads like hype.

Set boundaries so authenticity doesn't become oversharing. Decide what parts of your life are public, what's private, and what requires a pause before you post. Boundaries protect your values and keep your brand sustainable.

Finally, schedule a quarterly brand check-in. Ask: (1) Do my recent posts reflect my stated values? (2) Did any partnership feel off-brand? (3) What feedback kept coming up? Keep what aligns, cut what doesn't, and adjust your pillars as you grow. Consistent, small adjustments will keep your brand clear, credible, and truly yours.

Protecting Your Brand's Reputation

Your personal brand's reputation is one of your most valuable assets. How you manage it online and offline can significantly impact your relationship with fans, sponsors, and the wider community. This section covers essential strategies to monitor, protect, and enhance your brand reputation effectively.

Monitoring Your Online Presence

Regularly Google yourself: Set up alerts or reminders to check what content appears when your name or brand is searched.

Use social media monitoring tools: Platforms like Hootsuite or Mention can track brand mentions across multiple social channels and websites.

Keep an eye on comments and reviews: Stay aware of feedback on your posts, merchandise, or business dealings.

Check for unauthorized use: Monitor if others are using your name, image, or logo without permission.

Proactively monitoring helps you catch potential issues early and identify opportunities to engage positively.

Handling Negative Feedback or Controversy Professionally

Respond calmly and promptly: Acknowledge concerns respectfully without reacting emotionally or defensively.

Take conversations offline when appropriate: Offer to discuss sensitive issues privately to avoid public escalation.

Apologize if needed: Owning mistakes shows maturity and can defuse tensions.

Avoid prolonging disputes: Know when to disengage and focus on positive messaging.

Use a crisis plan: Prepare in advance how you and your team will handle significant reputation challenges.

Turning negative situations into opportunities to demonstrate accountability and growth can strengthen your brand.

Strategies to Maintain and Grow Your Brand's Positive Image

Be authentic and consistent: Consistently share your values, accomplishments, and behind-the-scenes moments that humanize your brand.

Show gratitude: Recognize fans, sponsors, teammates, and community supporters regularly.

Engage positively with your audience: Respond to comments, messages, and collaborate with other influencers or brands.

Give back: Partner with charitable causes or community events aligned with your values.

Keep evolving: Refresh your brand messaging and content to stay relevant and exciting.

A strong reputation is built through ongoing care, genuine interactions, and purposeful actions. Cultivating goodwill today creates lasting value for your brand tomorrow.

Managing your brand's reputation is a continuous process. With attentive monitoring, professional handling of challenges, and a focus on positive growth, you'll build a resilient brand that stands out both on and off the field.

How Branding Impacts NIL Deals and Sponsorships

Your personal brand is a powerful tool for attracting NIL opportunities, endorsements, and sponsorship deals. A well-crafted, authentic, and consistent brand makes you more appealing to potential partners, and strategic outreach can turn relationships into ongoing collaborations.

Brand recognition: Sponsors seek athletes whose name, image, and story resonate with their target audience. A recognizable and positive brand attracts more sponsorship interest.

Alignment of values: Your personal brand should align with potential partners' values and target markets. For example, an athlete passionate about community service may attract sponsorships from local businesses or nonprofits.

Professional image: Consistent visuals, messaging, and campaign collaborations demonstrate professionalism and reliability, making sponsors more confident in partnering with you.

Influence and reach: A strong, engaged social media presence and compelling content expand your influence, increasing sponsorship value.

Tips for Professional Outreach and Partnership Management

Build a media kit: Prepare a professional media kit that highlights your athletic achievements, brand story, audience demographics, social media stats, and past collaborations. Make it easy for sponsors to see your value.

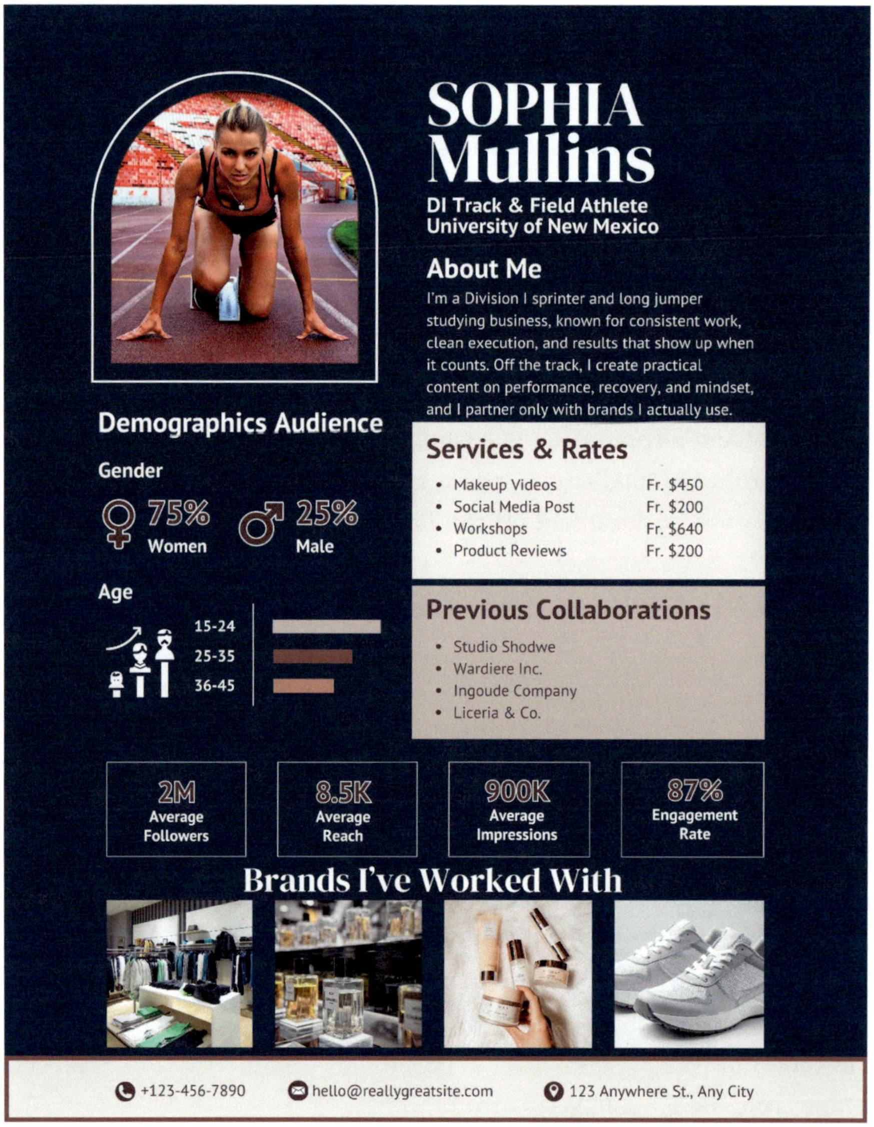

Identify ideal partners: Research brands and companies that match your personal brand and audience. Tailor your outreach to demonstrate how you can add value.

Craft personalized pitches: Send well-crafted, respectful messages that show you've researched the brand, explain why you're a good fit, and propose specific ideas for collaboration.

Be professional and timely: Respond promptly to inquiries, deliver on commitments, and maintain a positive attitude in all communications.

Leverage social proof: Showcase past partnerships, testimonials, or media coverage to build credibility.

Manage partnerships proactively: Keep sponsors informed about your activities, share campaign results, and suggest future opportunities to deepen the relationship.

Your personal brand is your most valuable asset in attracting sponsorships and NIL deals. By consistently maintaining an authentic, professional image and strategically reaching out to aligned partners, you can build mutually beneficial relationships that elevate your reputation, generate income, and expand your influence both on and off the field.

Identifying Your Brand's Target Audience

Your brand is strongest when it speaks to a specific group of people who actually care about what you offer. That can include fans who connect with your sport and personality, local or national businesses looking for believable endorsements, youth athletes (and their parents) who see you as a model to follow, and sponsors whose values line up with yours. Knowing exactly who you're talking to lets you tailor your message, choose the right platforms, and create offers that land.

Create & Segment Simple Audience Personas

Start by splitting your audience into a few tiers: a primary group you serve first, a secondary group you still support, and a tertiary group that's nice to reach when it happens. Then sketch 1–3 quick personas that feel real -- give each one an age range, where they live, what they care about, the problems they run into, where they spend time online, and what they want from you. Add a line of proof -- why you can actually help them (your story, consistent content, results, or testimonials). This doesn't need to be fancy; it just needs to be specific enough to guide your posts, outreach, and deals.

Match Audience → Offer → Channel

- ❖ Fans & youth athletes: how-to clips, training routines, Q&As, camps/clinics
  - ➢ Channels: TikTok, Instagram Reels, YouTube Shorts, in-person clinics

- ❖ Local businesses: community presence, family-friendly image, reliable deliverables
  - ➢ Channels: Instagram posts/stories, in-store appearances, local press

- ❖ Alumni & boosters (brand-safe): professionalism, academics, community work
  - ➢ Channels: LinkedIn, alumni newsletters, university-approved events

- ❖ Regional/national brands: clean storytelling, analytics, consistent creative
  - ➢ Channels: Instagram + YouTube, media kit, email outreach, agency platforms

Clarify the Value Your Brand Provides to Each Audience

Spell out, in one sentence per audience, what they get from you. For fans: practical tips and an honest look behind the scenes. For youth and parents: simple drills, mindset habits, and school-life balance that fit busy schedules. For local businesses: content plus appearances that reliably move attention toward their storefront. For sponsors: brand-safe content, clear deliverables, clean usage rights, and measurable results. If you can't explain the value quickly, the offer needs work.

Create Concrete, Lasting Message Pillars

Choose 3–4 pillars you'll repeat across platforms so people know what to expect:

- ❖ Performance & preparation

- ❖ Academics & routines

- ❖ Community & service

- ❖ Health & recovery

- ❖ Entrepreneurship & NIL lessons

Use Real Data to Find (and Keep) Your People

Don't guess -- check platform analytics to see which posts get saves and shares, when your audience is online, and where they live. Read your DMs and comments for repeated questions -- that's content and product ideas (plus, by answering those questions, you're adding real value for your target audience). Run quick polls to ask what they want next. Offline, tap into school channels, alumni groups, local chambers, and youth leagues. The more you listen, the sharper your targeting gets.

Measure Your Brand's Fit and Make Necessary Adjustments

Engagement rate rising = message & audience fit. If likes, comments, and saves as a percentage of followers are climbing, your voice, topics, and format are landing. Double down on the pillars that drive the bump, post at the times your audience is most active, and replicate winning structures. Track per-post engagement, not just totals, so you can spot exactly what to scale. But, remember to always be authentic in what you post so that your brand is a true reflection of you.

Saves, replies, and click-throughs = real utility. Saves mean "I'll need this later," replies mean "this sparked a conversation," and CTR means "I'm taking action." That combo tells you your content is useful, not just entertaining. Create sequels or mini-series on those topics, add simple next steps (checklist, template, drill), and tighten links so you can see which posts actually drive traffic, signups, or sales.

Inbound from the right brands = positioning on point. When companies that match your values and audience start contacting you, your bio, visuals, and content signals are aligned. Respond with a clean media kit (story, stats, audience, case studies), a rate card, and example deliverables. If outreach skews off-brand, refine your pillars, clarify your "who I serve" line, prune mismatched posts, and showcase partnerships that reflect where you want to go.

Choosing The Right Name For Your Business

Tips for Selecting a Memorable, Marketable Name

Your business name is often the first impression you make on fans, sponsors, and partners. Choosing a name that is catchy, easy to remember, and reflects your brand is essential for long-term success. Here are some tips to guide you:

- Keep it short and simple: Names that are easy to spell and pronounce stick better in people's minds. Shorter business names allow for shorter domain names, which are better when creating your website (they are more memorable and effective for marketing).

- Be unique: Stand out from competitors with a name that's distinct and not overly generic.

- Make it meaningful: The name should reflect your personality, values, or what your business offers.

- Avoid trends: Pick a timeless name to avoid it becoming outdated.

- Test it out: Say it aloud, ask friends for feedback, and imagine how it would look on merchandise or social media.

Checking Availability and Trademarks

Before you settle on a name, it's critical to check if it's legally available. To do that, search the USPTO database. The United States Patent and Trademark Office website lets you see if your desired name or similar ones are registered trademarks. Once you determine that your name and trademark are available, you can file to protect them with the USPTO.

You'll also want to check to ensure the business name is available as a domain name for your website. Websites like GoDaddy.com allow you to check for domain name availability, and provide you with alternatives if the specific name you want is already taken. If the domain name you want is taken, you can contact the owner of the domain and negotiate a sale of the name. Having a matching domain name and business name strengthens your online presence and legitimacy.

The same goes with social media handles for your business. Before you settle on a business name, look to see if the name (or a variation that works) is available on key social media platforms. It's best to secure consistent handles on all social media platforms for brand recognition.

Finally, you must also check with your state's business registry (often through the state's corporation commission) for your business name's availability. You can do a business name search for existing companies with that name.

Securing your business name prior to launching your business legally protects you from others using it and avoids costly rebranding later. Naming your business thoughtfully lays a sturdy foundation for all your branding and marketing efforts. Take your time, research thoroughly, and pick a name that truly represents who you are and where you want to go.

Protecting Your Brand: Trademarks, Logos, And Intellectual Property Basics

Protecting your brand is crucial to maintaining its value, credibility, and uniqueness. Understanding the different types of intellectual property (IP) and how to safeguard your assets helps you prevent unauthorized use and builds a strong foundation for your athlete business.

What Can Be Trademarked?

Brand Names

This is the word or phrase people use to identify you or your product. Strong names are distinctive (think made-up or unexpected words), not generic ("Sports Drink") or purely descriptive ("Fast Fitness Coaching"). The more distinctive the name, the easier it is to protect. Before you fall in love with a name, search the USPTO and do a basic web/social handle check to avoid conflicts. You'll register the name for specific goods/services (your "classes"), and you'll need to show actual use in commerce.

Logos and Symbols

These are the stylized marks, icons, and lockups that visually represent your brand. A simple, unique design is easier to protect than something that looks like every other shield, swoosh, or initials in your conference. When you file, you can protect the exact stylized logo

and, separately, the plain-word name -- both matter. Keep editable files and consistent usage so your look builds recognition (and evidence) over time.

Slogans or Taglines

Short phrases that capture your promise or vibe (e.g., a mantra on content, merch, or your site). Not every phrase is registrable -- common or purely descriptive wording is weak -- but a distinctive, memorable line can be protected if you actually use it to brand your goods/services, not just as decoration. Put the tagline on packaging, headers, or product pages so there's a clear "source" connection.

Mascots or Characters

A recurring illustrated figure, avatar, or persona tied to your identity can function as a trademark if people see it and think "that's you." Use it consistently on merch tags, videos, and promos so it signals source (not just fan art). If the character has a backstory or name, protect those elements too. This is also a spot where copyright and trademark can overlap -- copyright covers the artwork; trademark covers it as a brand identifier.

Some Sounds and Colors

Non-traditional marks are possible when they're truly distinctive. A short audio logo (a few notes, a unique sting) can be a sound mark if audiences connect it to you. Single colors or color placements can be protected trade dress in narrow contexts when they aren't functional and have "acquired distinctiveness" (people recognize the color as you). These take more proof -- consistent, long-term use and evidence that the public links the sound or color to your brand.

Trademark vs. Copyright vs. Patents

Trademark

Trademarks (or "mark") protect the things that tell people who the source is, such as names, logos, slogans, even distinctive packaging ("trade dress"). Protection grows out of use in commerce (actually selling goods/services under the mark), and registration with the USPTO strengthens your rights. You'll pick classes (categories) for what you sell, and what you're guarding against is likelihood of confusion, that is, someone using a mark close enough that buyers might think it's you. You can use ™ without registration; ® is for registered marks only. Strong marks are distinctive or made-up; weak marks are generic or purely descriptive. One more practical tip: printing a phrase huge across the front of a shirt can be treated as decoration, not a source identifier; if a slogan matters, also use it where it clearly functions as branding (hangtags, neck labels, product pages).

Copyright

Copyright protects the original creative content you make, such as photos, videos, graphics, music, written copy, or podcasts. It arises automatically when the work is fixed (saved/recorded), and it gives you exclusive rights to copy, distribute, adapt, display, and perform the work. Registration isn't required to own a copyright, but registering with the U.S. Copyright Office gives you big enforcement advantages (ability to sue, statutory damages, attorney's fees). Two areas to watch: (1) ownership: if a brand pays for a shoot, the contract may say they own it or get an exclusive license; read that section closely. (2) others' content: dropping a popular song or image into your video without a license can trigger takedowns or claims. Copyright protects the expression (your exact photo/video), not the idea behind it, and limited "fair use" exists but is risky to assume without advice.

Patent

Patents cover inventions, such as new, useful, and non-obvious products, processes, or designs (think a novel training device, a performance-enhancing apparel feature, or a unique bottle design). Utility patents protect how something works; design patents protect how it looks. This path is more technical and expensive: you typically file a provisional to hold your spot, then a full application within 12 months, and you must keep the invention non-public (use NDAs) until you file. Patents are less common for personal branding, but if you create a product with real novelty, patenting can secure an avenue for licensing or sales. Ideas alone aren't patentable; you need a concrete, teachable implementation. Terms are long (generally ~20 years from filing for utility; 15 for design), but only if you follow the process and keep fees/current.

Safeguarding your intellectual property is an investment in your brand's future. Understanding these basics empowers you to build a strong, protected presence that can grow and thrive in the competitive world of sports and business.

Step-by-Step Guide To Apply For A Trademark (USPTO)

Applying for a trademark through the United States Patent and Trademark Office (USPTO) is a key step in legally protecting your personal brand, logo, or business name. Here's a detailed guide to help you prepare, file, and avoid common pitfalls along the way.

Preparing and Researching Your Trademark Application

Choose a strong trademark: Pick a name, logo, or slogan that is distinctive and easy to protect. Avoid generic or descriptive terms.

Conduct a thorough search: Use the USPTO's Trademark Electronic Search System (TESS) to check if your desired trademark or anything similar is already registered or pending. This helps avoid conflicts or infringement.

Define your goods/services: Clearly describe the products or services your trademark will represent, using USPTO's Acceptable Identification of Goods and Services manual as a guide.

Filing Process Walkthrough

Create a USPTO account: Visit uspto.gov to register for an account in the Trademark Electronic Application System (TEAS).

Select your application form: For most personal brand trademarks, the TEAS Standard or TEAS Plus forms are appropriate.

Submit your trademark specimen: Provide a clear example showing your trademark in use (e.g., product labels, website screenshots).

Pay the filing fee: Fees typically range from $250 to $350 per class of goods/services.

Review your application: After submission, the USPTO will assign an examining attorney to review your application for compliance and conflicts.

Respond to office actions: If the examiner has questions or objections, respond promptly with clarifications or arguments.

Publication and registration: If approved, your trademark is published for opposition. If no challenges arise, you receive your registration certificate.

Common Pitfalls to Avoid

Skipping the trademark search: Failing to check for existing trademarks can result in rejection or costly legal disputes.

Poor specimen selection: Submitting unclear or inappropriate examples of your trademark use can delay approval.

Vague or incomplete descriptions: Ambiguous descriptions of goods/services can cause office actions.

Ignoring deadlines: Missing response deadlines can result in application abandonment.

Applying for a trademark is a powerful way to protect your brand's identity and create lasting value. Being thorough and attentive throughout this process will help your application succeed and secure your brand's future.

Hiring An Attorney Or DIY Trademark Filing?

When protecting your brand through trademark registration, one of the important decisions you'll face is whether to handle the process yourself (DIY), use an online service like LegalZoom, or hire a professional trademark attorney. Understanding the pros, cons, costs, and risks of each option will help you make the best choice for your situation.

DIY Trademark Filing

Many entrepreneurs, including college athletes, choose to file trademark applications themselves through the USPTO website's Trademark Electronic Application System (TEAS). The DIY route gives you full control and saves money by avoiding legal fees.

Pros:

- Lowest cost: only pay USPTO filing fees (usually $250 to $350 per class).

- ❖ You learn the process firsthand, gaining valuable knowledge about intellectual property.
- ❖ Complete control over your application timeline and content.

Cons:

- ❖ The trademark process is complex, with legal terminology and strict procedural rules.
- ❖ Small mistakes, incorrect descriptions, or incomplete applications can delay approval or lead to rejection.
- ❖ Responding to USPTO office actions or legal objections can be challenging without expertise.

To assist with the DIY approach, Hopkins Law Sports Management offers a specialized workshop that guides athletes through each step of DIY trademark filing. This workshop helps you navigate searches, applications, and responses, minimizing errors and increasing your chances of success.

Using Online Legal Services (e.g., LegalZoom)

Online platforms offer a middle ground: providing guided applications, document review, and some legal advice at a lower cost than full legal representation.

Pros:

- ❖ Simplifies the process with easy-to-use forms and instructions.
- ❖ Usually less expensive than hiring a trademark attorney.
- ❖ Can save time compared to fully DIY if you're unfamiliar with the trademark system.

Cons:

- ❖ Services vary widely in quality and depth of support.

- ❖ May not provide personalized advice specific to your brand or complex legal issues.
- ❖ Still a risk of errors if you do not fully understand trademark law.

Hiring a Trademark Attorney

A trademark lawyer offers full-service, expert legal guidance through each phase of your trademark registration.

Pros:

- ❖ Knowledgeable about USPTO procedures, helping avoid common pitfalls.
- ❖ Can conduct comprehensive trademark searches and assess risks.
- ❖ Craft application details precisely to maximize chances of approval.
- ❖ Handles complex responses to office actions.
- ❖ Provides ongoing advice about enforcement, licensing, and brand protection.

Cons:

- ❖ Higher cost, often from several hundred to a few thousand dollars.
- ❖ May take more time upfront due to detailed legal work.
- ❖ Cost, Time, and Risk Comparison

Option	Cost Range	Time Commitment	Risk of Errors or Rejection
DIY Filing	\$250–\$350	High	High
Online Legal Services	\$300–\$800+	Medium	Medium
Hiring an Attorney	\$800–\$3,000+	Low to medium	Low, expert handling

Making an informed choice about trademark filing balances your budget, timeline, and comfort with legal procedures. Whether you choose DIY with the help of workshops like those offered by Hopkins Law Sports Management, use an online service, or hire an attorney, protecting your brand is an essential investment in your future.

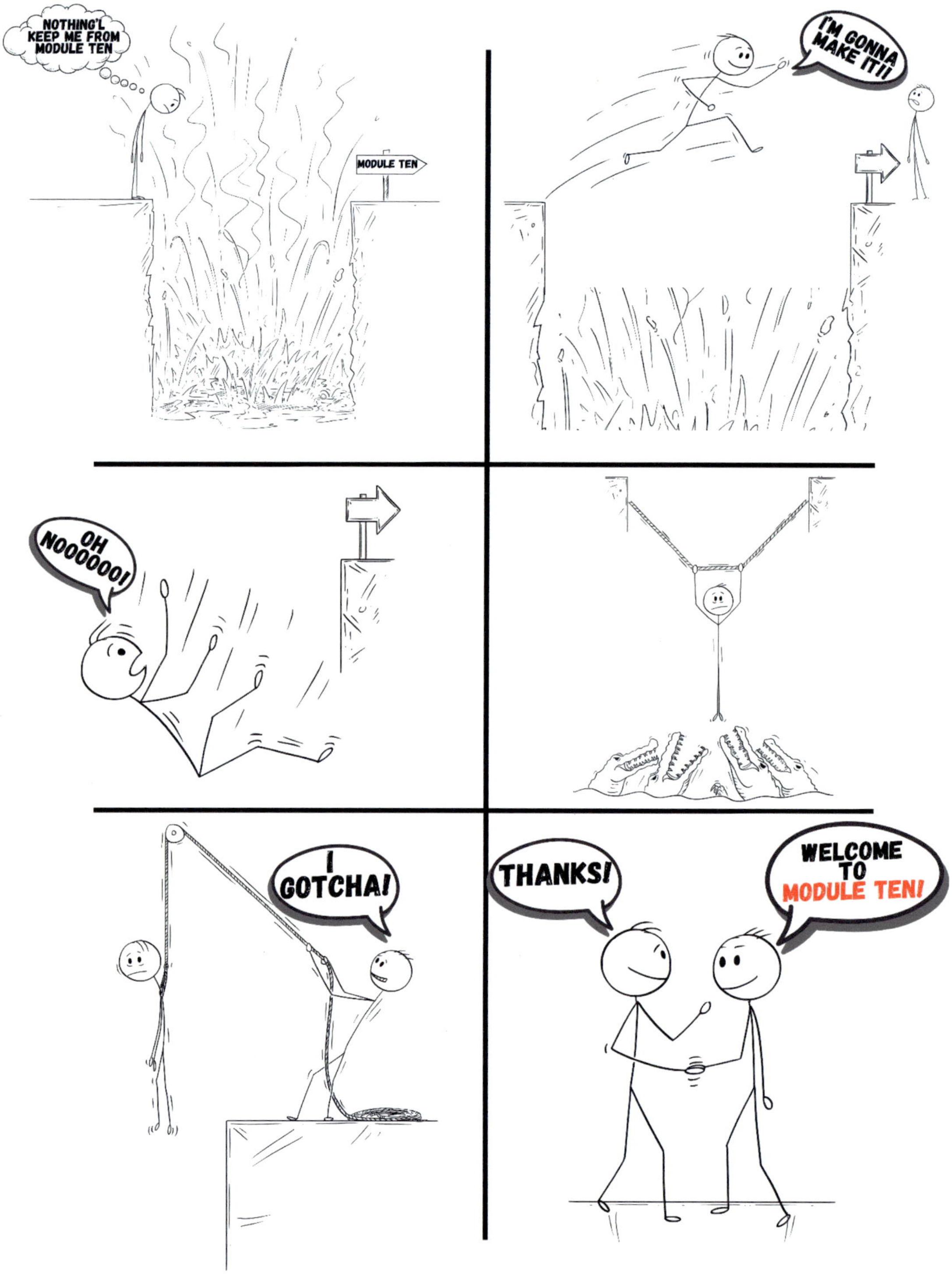

MODULE TEN

HANDS-ON NIL AND REV-SHARE WORKSHOP--LET'S GET YOU SET UP!

This workshop series is designed to guide college athletes step-by-step through the practical tasks covered in this book. Each part of the workshop focuses on key set-up actions such as forming a business entity, opening bank accounts, trademark registrations, and building your digital presence. By participating in the workshop, you'll receive hands-on support, live demonstrations, templates, and resources to confidently manage your NIL and Rev-Share opportunities.

Workshop Schedule and Topics

1. Getting Your EIN and Business Formation

<u>What it covers</u>: Learn how to apply for your Employer Identification Number (EIN) from the IRS, choose the right business structure (sole proprietorship, LLC, etc.), and register your business.

<u>What HLO offers</u>: Live walkthrough of IRS application, explanation of business structure pros and cons, and downloadable forms.

2. Setting Up Your Business Bank Account

<u>What it covers</u>: Step-by-step guide to opening a dedicated business bank account to separate personal and business finances.

<u>What HLO offers</u>: Checklist of required documents, tips for selecting banks, and best practices for bookkeeping.

3. Trademark Basics and DIY Filing

<u>What it covers</u>: Understand trademark essentials and how to conduct your own search and application through the USPTO.

What HLO offers: Access to the DIY Trademark Workshop with live demonstrations of the USPTO system, sample searches, and application reviews.

4. Branding and Intellectual Property Protection

What it covers: Explore how to define your brand identity, protect your logos and content, and basics of copyright and licensing.

What HLO offers: Brand identity worksheets, IP protection checklists, and guidance on licensing opportunities.

5. Building Your Digital Presence: Social Media & Website Setup

What it covers: Learn to set up professional social media profiles and an effective personal website aligned with your brand.

What HLO offers: Website planning templates, social media best practice guides, and setup demonstrations.

6. Understanding Contracts and Common Pitfalls

What it covers: Get familiar with contract basics, key clauses, red flags, and how to avoid common mistakes in NIL and Rev-Share deals.

What HLO offers: Sample contract reviews, negotiation tips, and Q&A sessions.

7. Financial Tools and Tax Basics

What it covers: Cover basics of retirement accounts, budgeting NIL income, tax obligations, and managing financial planning.

What HLO offers: Personalized budgeting templates, guidance on opening retirement accounts, and introduction to tax resources.

Workshop Format

- Interactive sessions with live demonstrations
- Q&A and individual consultations
- Actionable handouts and resource lists
- Follow-up support and check-ins to track progress

These workshops are tailored to empower college athletes with the practical skills to set a strong foundation for financial success and brand growth while staying compliant and protected. By attending, athletes transform knowledge from this book into real-world action.

MODULE ELEVEN

TEMPLATES, FORMS, AND WORKSHEETS TO HELP GUIDE YOU

Here's what Module Eleven is (and isn't). You're getting sample forms, checklists, and model clauses -- plus reference documents like the House Settlement text -- to help you see what a clean, compliant NIL or Rev-Share agreement looks like on paper. Use these materials to understand structure, spot key terms (payment schedules, deliverables, termination, dispute resolution), and build your own first draft. Treat them as teaching tools and starting points, not one-size-fits-all contracts. Every deal is different, and your facts, school policies, and state law matter.

Very important: nothing in this module is legal advice, and you shouldn't sign or rely on any template without having it reviewed by a qualified attorney. Laws vary by state, conferences issue their own policies, schools add overlays, and tax consequences can change the economics of what looks good on the surface. When you adapt any document, keep version history, track redlines, and save all attachments (exhibits, deliverable schedules, W-9/1099 info). Before you execute anything, run it past your attorney (and, where relevant, your CPA and compliance office) to confirm the terms fit your situation and keep you eligible, compliant, and protected.

Sample NIL Contract

LICENSE AGREEMENT

This **Legal Agreement ("**Agreement") is made and entered into and effective as of January 1, 2025 ("Effective Date") and by and between Sports Drink, LLC ("Company") and Student-Athlete ("Athlete").

1. **License, Use, and Limitations**
   a. Grant of License: The Athlete hereby grants to the Company a non-exclusive license to use the Athlete's Name, Image, and Likeness (collectively, "NIL"), including their full name, photographs, and video likeness, solely for the purpose of promoting the Company's sports drink products (the "Products") in advertisements and on product packaging.
   b. Ownership and Control: The Athlete retains full ownership of their NIL. The Company may not alter the Athlete's NIL (e.g., edit photos or videos) beyond basic resizing without the Athlete's written consent.
   c. Grant of Exclusive License: During the term of this Agreement, the Athlete will not grant any other person, company, or brand the right to use their NIL to promote sports drinks or related products ("Competitive Products") , and Athlete will refrain from publicly purchasing, mentioning, or interacting with any Competitive Products. Competitive Products will be defined as and limited to: Gatorade, Powerade, Body Armor, and Propel.
   d. Scope of Use: The Company may use the Athlete's NIL in print ads, social media posts, and on Product cans and bottles sold in the United States. Any other use, including different products or regions, requires the Athlete's prior written approval.
   e. Perpetual Use of Name, Image, and Likeness: Company shall have the right to use in perpetuity, such advertising materials for internal purposes such as historical, educational or commemorative purposes, provided any such use shall not suggest or imply a continued endorsement or sponsorship relationship between Athlete and Company.
   f. Term of Use: This license is effective from June 1, 2025, to May 31, 2026, unless terminated earlier as provided in this Agreement ("Term"). The Company may not use the Athlete's NIL after this term without a new written agreement.
   g. Approval of Advertising: Athlete will be given 3 days to approve of any use of their Name, Image, and Likeness in advertising and promotion of the Company's Product.
2. **Student-Athlete Duties and Obligations**
   a. Services:
      i. Athlete shall provide the following services to the Company during the Term of this Agreement:
         1. 5 Instagram posts with Products with a link to the product website
         2. 10 Instagram story posts with videos and/or pictures of the Product
         3. Autograph 1,000 bottles of the Product for a promotional giveaway

b. Non-Disparagement: The Athlete shall not (a) knowingly make any damaging or harmful statements—spoken, written, or online—about Company and Company's products; or (b) do anything which might reasonably be considered to be immoral, scandalous or obscene, or otherwise damage the reputation of the Company during the term of this Agreement.

c. Non-Compete: The Athlete agrees not to engage in or endorse any business that competes with the Company during the term of this Agreement and for one year after termination. This includes the use of the Athlete's NIL with any sports drink or related competitor without prior written consent from Company.

3. Company Duties and Obligations

a. Payment and Compensation:

i. Company shall provide Athlete $10,000 for Student-Athlete's NIL and the services required under Section 2a of this Agreement.

ii. Company shall pay Athlete within 5 business days of this Agreement being signed.

4. Termination

a. Either party shall have the right to immediately terminate this Agreement during the Term if the other Party materially breaches its duties and obligations and such breach remains uncured.

b. Either party may terminate this Agreement for any reason at any time by providing 14 days written notice to the other party.

c. Termination for NCAA or School Compliance: Company acknowledges and agrees that this Agreement is subject to the approval of Athlete's postsecondary educational institution (or other academic institution) as is, or may be, required by applicable state law or governmental mandate.

5. Indemnification

a. Company agrees to be solely responsible for, defend, hold harmless and indemnify Athlete from and against third party claims, demands, suits, losses, damages, and expenses thereof (including reasonable attorney's fees) resulting from this Agreement, including: (i) Company's negligent acts or omissions; (ii) a material breach of this Agreement by Company; (iii) any Company's advertising, promotion or publicity proven to utilize false, misleading or deceptive advertising, or any unpermitted usage of Athlete's NIL; and (v) any violation of applicable law, rule or regulation by Company in performing its obligations hereunder.

b. Athlete agrees to defend, hold harmless and indemnify Company, from and against any third party claims, demands, suits, losses, damages, and expenses thereof (including reasonable attorney's fees) arising out of, or in any way connected to: (i) any negligent actions or omissions of Athlete in the performance of the services under this Agreement; and (ii) any material breach of this Agreement by the Athlete.

6. Miscellaneous

a. Independent Contractor Relationship: Athlete shall be considered an independent contractor. Nothing in this Agreement shall be construed as establishing an employer/employee relationship. Athlete shall be solely responsible for the payment of all income taxes on the compensation received pursuant to this Agreement.

b. Force Majeure: Neither the Athlete nor the Company will be responsible for failing to meet their obligations under this Agreement if an extraordinary event beyond their control—like earthquakes, floods, pandemics, government shutdowns, or riots—prevents them from performing, such as the Athlete NIL for the Company's protein shake campaign ("Campaign").
c. No assignment: The rights, duties and obligations of Athlete set forth in this Agreement may not be assigned, delegated, or otherwise transferred in any way or in whole or in part, whether voluntarily or involuntarily, without the express written consent of Company. This Agreement shall inure to the benefit of any permitted successors and permitted assigns and shall be binding upon any such successors and assigns.
d. Governing Law/Arbitration: This Agreement will be governed by and construed in accordance with the laws of the State of Oregon without giving effect to its principles of the conflict of laws. If a dispute arises under this Agreement which cannot first be resolved through good faith negotiations, the dispute will be submitted to arbitration and resolved by a single arbitrator. The award or decision rendered by the arbitrator is final, binding and conclusive and any court may enter judgment upon the award.
e. Confidentiality: The terms and conditions of this Agreement are confidential, and, therefore, shall not be made available to any third parties without the prior written consent of the parties to this Agreement, with the exception only of disclosure to such party's agents, attorneys, accountants, representatives, or employees, and except as may be required by law or applicable legal proceeding.
f. Notices: Any notice required under this Agreement, such as termination, payment disputes, or changes to the use of the Athlete's NIL, must be in writing and sent by email, certified mail, or a recognized delivery service (e.g., FedEx).
g. Entire Agreement: This Agreement constitutes the entire understanding between the Athlete and Company and cannot be altered or modified except by an agreement in writing signed by both parties. Upon its execution, this Agreement shall supersede all prior negotiations, understandings and agreements, whether oral or written, and such prior agreements shall thereupon be null and void and without further legal effect.

IN WITNESS WHEREOF, the Parties hereto have caused this Agreement to be executed as of the Effective Date by their respective officers thereunto duly authorized.

ATHLETE

By____________________

Name:

Title:

COMPANY

By____________________

Name:

Title:

LLC Formation Docs (Articles of Incorporation, Statement of Information, LLC Operating Agreement)

Secretary of State **Articles of Incorporation of a General Stock Corporation**	**ARTS-GS**

IMPORTANT — Read Instructions before completing this form.

Filing Fee – $100.00

Copy Fees – First page $1.00; each attachment page $0.50; Certification Fee - $5.00

Note: Corporations may have to pay minimum $800 tax to the California Franchise Tax Board each year. For more information, go to *https://www.ftb.ca.gov*.

This Space For Office Use Only

1. Corporate Name (Go to *www.sos.ca.gov/business/be/name-availability* for general corporate name requirements and restrictions.)

The name of the corporation is ____

____

2. Business Addresses (Enter the **complete** business addresses.)

a. Initial Street Address of Corporation - **Do not list a P.O. Box**	City (no abbreviations)	State	Zip Code
b. Initial Mailing Address of Corporation, **if different than item 2a**	City (no abbreviations)	State	Zip Code

3. Service of Process (Must provide either Individual **OR** Corporation.)

INDIVIDUAL – Complete Items 3a and 3b only. Must include agent's full name and California street address.

a. California Agent's First Name (if agent is **not** a corporation)	Middle Name	Last Name	Suffix
b. Street Address (if agent is **not** a corporation) - **Do not enter a P.O. Box**	City (no abbreviations)	State **CA**	Zip Code

CORPORATION – Complete Item 3c. Only include the name of the registered agent Corporation.

c. California Registered Corporate Agent's Name (if agent is a corporation) – Do not complete Item 3a or 3b

4. Shares (Enter the **number of shares** the corporation is authorized to issue. **Do not** leave blank or enter zero (0).)

This corporation is authorized to issue only one class of shares of stock.
The total number of shares which this corporation is authorized to issue is ______________________.

5. Purpose Statement (Do not alter the Purpose Statement.)

The purpose of the corporation is to engage in any lawful act or activity for which a corporation may be organized under the General Corporation Law of California other than the banking business, the trust company business or the practice of a profession permitted to be incorporated by the California Corporations Code.

6. Read and Sign Below (This form must be signed by each incorporator. **See instructions for signature requirements.**)

______________________________ ______________________________

Signature Type or Print Name

ARTS-GS (REV06/2019)

L

State of California
Secretary of State

STATEMENT OF INFORMATION
(Limited Liability Company)

Filing Fee $20.00. If amendment, see instructions.

IMPORTANT — READ INSTRUCTIONS BEFORE COMPLETING THIS FORM

1. **LIMITED LIABILITY COMPANY NAME** (Please do not alter if name is preprinted.)

This Space For Filing Use Only

DUE DATE: [For forms preprinted by the Secretary of State.]

FILE NUMBER AND STATE OR PLACE OF ORGANIZATION

2. SECRETARY OF STATE FILE NUMBER	3. STATE OR PLACE OF ORGANIZATION

NO CHANGE STATEMENT

☐ If there has been no change in any of the information contained in the last Statement of Information filed with the Secretary of State, check the box and proceed **to Item 13**.

If there have been any changes to the information contained in the last Statement of Information filed, or no Statement of Information has been previously filed, this form must be completed in its entirety.

COMPLETE ADDRESSES FOR THE FOLLOWING (Do not abbreviate the name of the city. Items 4 and 5 cannot be P.O. Boxes.)

4. STREET ADDRESS OF PRINCIPAL EXECUTIVE OFFICE	CITY AND STATE		ZIP CODE
5. CALIFORNIA OFFICE WHERE RECORDS ARE MAINTAINED **(DOMESTIC ONLY)**	CITY	STATE **CA**	ZIP CODE

NAME AND COMPLETE ADDRESS OF THE CHIEF EXECUTIVE OFFICER, IF ANY

6. NAME	ADDRESS	CITY AND STATE	ZIP CODE

NAME AND COMPLETE ADDRESS OF ANY MANAGER OR MANAGERS, OR IF NONE HAVE BEEN APPOINTED OR ELECTED, PROVIDE THE NAME AND ADDRESS OF EACH MEMBER (Attach additional pages, if necessary.)

7. NAME	ADDRESS	CITY AND STATE	ZIP CODE
8. NAME	ADDRESS	CITY AND STATE	ZIP CODE
9. NAME	ADDRESS	CITY AND STATE	ZIP CODE

AGENT FOR SERVICE OF PROCESS (If the agent is an individual, the agent must reside in California and Item 11 must be completed with a California address. If the agent is a corporation, the agent must have on file with the California Secretary of State a certificate pursuant to Corporations Code section 1505 and Item 11 must be left blank.)

10. NAME OF AGENT FOR SERVICE OF PROCESS

11. ADDRESS OF AGENT FOR SERVICE OF PROCESS IN CALIFORNIA, **IF AN INDIVIDUAL**	CITY	STATE **CA**	ZIP CODE

TYPE OF BUSINESS

12. DESCRIBE THE TYPE OF BUSINESS OF THE LIMITED LIABILITY COMPANY

13. THE INFORMATION CONTAINED HEREIN IS TRUE AND CORRECT.

TYPE OR PRINT NAME OF PERSON COMPLETING THE FORM	SIGNATURE	TITLE	DATE

LLC-12R (REV 03/2007) APPROVED BY SECRETARY OF STATE

Sample LLC Operating Agreement

OPERATING AGREEMENT

FOR

The undersigned, as sole member and manager of the Company does hereby enter into this Operating Agreement for the above-named, Limited Liability Company, hereinafter referred to as the "Company." This company shall be owned by

I
Contract

This Operating Agreement is a contract between its parties and is enforceable by the Company against any member who violates its terms. All members, past, present and future must sign this Operating Agreement as a condition of membership.

II
Office

The principal office of the Company is located at
The Company may have such other offices, either within or without the state as the members may designate or as the business of the Company may require. The registered office of the Company required by the laws of the State of New Jersey to be maintained in the state may be, but need not be, identical with the principal office, and may be changed from time to time by the members.

III
Purpose

The purpose for which the Company is organized is the conduct of all lawful business purposes for which it is formed.

IV
Duration of the Company

The Company shall commence immediately, upon signing of this Operating Agreement, and shall continue pursuant to the term specified in the documents filed with the state unless terminated sooner by operation of law or by agreement among the members.

V
Capital Contributions

The undersigned member(s) agree to share in all post-formation capital contributions, profits, and surplus of the Company according to the percentage of their membership or according to any other allocation the members, by unanimous vote, should agree upon. Each member owns an undivided interest in the business and Company as follows:

<u>Member</u>	<u>Percentage of Ownership</u>

VI

Additional Capital Contributions

The member(s) may contribute in proportionate amounts any additional capital deemed necessary for the operation of the Company, provided, however, that in the event that any member deems it advisable to refuse or fails to contribute such member's share of any or all of the additional capital, then the other members or any one of them may contribute the additional capital not paid in by such refusing member and shall receive therefore an increase in the entire Company in direct proportion to the said additional capital contributed. Unless otherwise agreed, the right to make up additional capital contributions of a refusing member shall be available in the same order as the right to purchase in the case of withdrawal or death of a member, as set forth in paragraphs XIV and XV.

VII
Division of Profits and Losses

Each of the member(s) shall own an interest in the Company as set forth in paragraph V, entitled "Capital Contributions", except as the same may hereafter vary or change as provided in paragraph VI, entitled "Additional Capital Contributions". All profits of the Company enterprise shall be shared in equal parts. No member(s) shall make any withdrawals from capital without prior approval of the Company.

VIII
Rights and Duties of the Parties

The entity is to be managed by its member(s). Company decisions and actions shall be decided by a majority vote of its members, at meetings regularly called with notice to all parties.

IX

Management Duties and Restrictions

No member shall, without the consent of the other members, endorse any note or act as an accommodation party, or otherwise become surety for any person in any transaction involved in the Company. Without the consent of the Company, no member shall on behalf of the Company borrow or lend money, or make, deliver or accept any commercial paper, or execute any mortgage, security agreement, bond or lease, or purchase or contract to purchase, or sell or contract to sell any property for or of the Company. No member shall, except with the consent of the other members, mortgage, grant a security interest in its share in the Company capital assets or property, or do any act detrimental to the best interests of the Company or which would make it impossible to carry on the ordinary purpose of the Company.

X
Banking and Financial Department

All funds of the Company shall be deposited in its name in such checking account or accounts as shall be designated by the member(s). All withdrawals there from are to be made upon checks which must be signed by the managing member or such person as the member(s) designate by unanimous vote.

XI
Books

The Company books shall be maintained at the Company offices, to be retained by the entity, and each member shall have access thereto. The books shall be kept on a calendar year basis, and shall be closed and balanced at the end of each fiscal year. Each of the parties to this Operating Agreement hereby covenants and agrees to cause all known business transactions pertaining to the purpose of the Company, to be entered properly and completely into said book. The Company will furnish annual financial statements to the members, and prepare tax returns in a timely manner.

XII
Insurance

The Company shall carry liability insurance in such amounts as deemed appropriate by the member(s) and as required by state law.

XIII
Voluntary Termination

If the Company is dissolved, the member(s) shall proceed with reasonable promptness to liquidate the Company. The assets of the Company shall be distributed in the following order:

1. To pay or provide for the payment of all Company liabilities to creditors other than members, and liquidating expenses and obligations;

2. To pay debts owing to members other than for capital and profits;

3. To pay debts owing to members in respect to capital; and

4. To pay debts owing to members in respect to profit.

XIV
Withdrawal of Member by Sale

Any member who shall be desirous of selling their share and interest in the Company shall give the right of first refusal to purchase said share and interest at the same price as being offered by a bona fide and qualified buyer to the other members, if any. All members electing to purchase (other than the selling member), and having the right to purchase, may purchase that percentage of share(s) being sold. The number of shares that can be purchased is calculated by dividing the member's respective percentage of the Company by the total percentage of shares of all members electing to purchase. The unanimous consent of all members is required for a member to sell their share to a non-member or for an assignee of a member's share to become a member.

XV
Death of a Member

In the event of the death of a member, then the deceased's heir or heirs shall be entitled to succeed to the economic share and interest of the deceased member. The Company shall, upon unanimous consent of the remaining members, as soon as practicable, provide a document by which the remaining members personally affirm and accept all the terms, conditions and provisions of this Operating Agreement binding themselves to continue the same business in writing. If no such heir or heirs exist or decline to succeed, and no such other members exist to elect to purchase the deceased shares, then the Company shall be dissolved in accordance with state law and any remaining assets shall be distributed to the deceased's estate.

XVI
Distribution

Prior to dissolution and at least annually as income has been received by the Company, accounts determined and tax returns filed, the member(s) shall determine funds available for distribution. Said distribution shall be made in equal amounts to the members.

XVII
Amendment of Operating Agreement

This Operating Agreement may be altered, amended or repealed and a new Operating Agreement may be adopted only by a majority vote of the membership at any annual, regular or special meeting of the members.

XVIII
Violation of This Operating Agreement

Any member who shall violate any of the terms, conditions, and provisions of this Operating Agreement shall keep and save harmless the Company property and shall also indemnify the other members from any and all claims, demands and actions of every kind and nature whatsoever which may arise out of or by reason of such violation of any terms and conditions of this Operating Agreement.

____

Managing Member

EIN Application Form

Form **SS-4** (Rev. December 2023) Department of the Treasury Internal Revenue Service

Application for Employer Identification Number

(For use by employers, corporations, partnerships, trusts, estates, churches, government agencies, Indian tribal entities, certain individuals, and others.)
See separate instructions for each line. Keep a copy for your records.
Go to *www.irs.gov/FormSS4* for instructions and the latest information.

OMB No. 1545-0003

EIN

Type or print clearly.

1 Legal name of entity (or individual) for whom the EIN is being requested

2 Trade name of business (if different from name on line 1) | 3 Executor, administrator, trustee, "care of" name

4a Mailing address (room, apt., suite no. and street, or P.O. box) | 5a Street address (if different) (Don't enter a P.O. box.)

4b City, state, and ZIP code (if foreign, see instructions) | 5b City, state, and ZIP code (if foreign, see instructions)

6 County and state where principal business is located

7a Name of responsible party | 7b SSN, ITIN, or EIN

8a Is this application for a limited liability company (LLC) (or a foreign equivalent)? . . . . ☐ Yes ☐ No

8b If 8a is "Yes," enter the number of LLC members . . . .

8c If 8a is "Yes," was the LLC organized in the United States? . . . . ☐ Yes ☐ No

9a **Type of entity** (check only one box). **Caution:** If 8a is "Yes," see the instructions for the correct box to check.

☐ Sole proprietor (SSN) ____________
☐ Partnership
☐ Corporation (enter form number to be filed) ____________
☐ Personal service corporation
☐ Church or church-controlled organization
☐ Other nonprofit organization (specify) ____________
☐ Other (specify)
☐ Estate (SSN of decedent) ____________
☐ Plan administrator (TIN) ____________
☐ Trust (TIN of grantor) ____________
☐ Military/National Guard
☐ State/local government
☐ Farmers' cooperative
☐ Federal government
☐ REMIC
☐ Indian tribal governments/enterprises

Group Exemption Number (GEN) if any

9b If a corporation, name the state or foreign country (if applicable) where incorporated | State | Foreign country

10 **Reason for applying** (check only one box)

☐ Started new business (specify type) ____________
☐ Hired employees (Check the box and see line 13.)
☐ Compliance with IRS withholding regulations
☐ Other (specify)
☐ Banking purpose (specify purpose) ____________
☐ Changed type of organization (specify new type) ____________
☐ Purchased going business
☐ Created a trust (specify type) ____________
☐ Created a pension plan (specify type) ____________

11 Date business started or acquired (month, day, year). See instructions.

12 Closing month of accounting year

13 Highest number of employees expected in the next 12 months (enter -0- if none). If no employees expected, skip line 14.

Agricultural	Household	Other

14 If you expect your employment tax liability to be $1,000 or less in a full calendar year **and** want to file Form 944 annually instead of Forms 941 quarterly, check here. (Your employment tax liability will generally be $1,000 or less if you expect to pay $5,000 or less, $6,536 or less if you're in a U.S. territory, in total wages.) If you don't check this box, you must file Form 941 for every quarter. ☐

15 First date wages or annuities were paid (month, day, year). **Note:** If applicant is a withholding agent, enter date income will first be paid to nonresident alien (month, day, year) . . . .

16 Check **one** box that best describes the principal activity of your business.

☐ Health care & social assistance ☐ Wholesale—agent/broker
☐ Construction ☐ Rental & leasing ☐ Transportation & warehousing ☐ Accommodation & food service ☐ Wholesale—other ☐ Retail
☐ Real estate ☐ Manufacturing ☐ Finance & insurance ☐ Other (specify)

17 Indicate principal line of merchandise sold, specific construction work done, products produced, or services provided.

18 Has the applicant entity shown on line 1 ever applied for and received an EIN? ☐ Yes ☐ No
If "Yes," write previous EIN here

Third Party Designee

Complete this section **only** if you want to authorize the named individual to receive the entity's EIN and answer questions about the completion of this form.

Designee's name | Designee's telephone number (include area code)

Address and ZIP code | Designee's fax number (include area code)

Under penalties of perjury, I declare that I have examined this application, and to the best of my knowledge and belief, it is true, correct, and complete. | Applicant's telephone number (include area code)

Name and title (type or print clearly)

Applicant's fax number (include area code)

Signature | Date

For Privacy Act and Paperwork Reduction Act Notice, see separate instructions. Cat. No. 16055N Form **SS-4** (Rev. 12-2023)

Budget & Income Tracker Spreadsheet

Monthly Budget

Starting balance: $1,000

+50%
Increase in total savings

$500
Saved this month

Expenses

Planned $950
Actual $1,000

Income

Planned $1,450
Actual $1,500

Expenses

	Planned	Actual	Diff.
Totals	*$950*	*$1,000*	*-$50*
Food	$0	$0	$0
Gifts	$0	$0	$0
Health/medical	$0	$0	$0
Home	$950	$1,000	-$50
Transportation	$0	$0	$0
Personal	$0	$0	$0
Pets	$0	$0	$0
Utilities	$0	$0	$0
Travel	$0	$0	$0
Debt	$0	$0	$0
Other	$0	$0	$0
Custom category 1	$0	$0	$0
Custom category 2	$0	$0	$0
Custom category 3	$0	$0	$0

Income

	Planned	Actual	Diff.
Totals	*$1,450*	*$1,500*	*+$50*
Savings	$0	$0	$0
Paycheck	$1,450	$1,500	+$50
Bonus	$0	$0	$0
Interest	$0	$0	$0
Other	$0	$0	$0
Custom category	$0	$0	$0

Invoice Template

College
Athlete, LLC

123 Anywhere st., Any City
123-456-7890

INVOICE

Invoice Number: #2913
Date: November 18, 2006
Due Date: November 26, 2016

BILL TO:

Business Owner
123 Anywhere st., Any City
+123-456-7890

Payment Method
Central Bank
Cedric Hopkins
123-456-7890

NO	ITEM DESRIPTION	PRICE	QTY	TOTAL
1	Social Media Posts Athlete will post sponsored content on Instagram & TikTok	$1000	1	$1000
2	Personal Appearance Athlete will personally appear at car dealership for one (1) hour	$3000	1	$3000
3	Autographs Athlete will sign at least fifty (50) items	$800	1	$800

Total	$4800
Tax	-
Discount	-
Sub Total	$4800

Term and Conditions:
All payments are made prior to either posting, appearing, or signing

Cedric Hopkins

Cedric Hopkins
College Athlete, LLC

Trademark Application

- Visit https://www.uspto.gov/sites/default/files/trademarks/teas/new_teas.pdf for the complete trademark application (page shown for reference)

United States Patent and Trademark Office
Trademark Electronic Application System - TEAS Application

Navigation History: Instruction > **Applicant** > Mark > Goods/Services/Filing Basis > Attorney/Dom. Rep./Correspondence > Fee/Signature

Under the Paperwork Reduction Act of 1995 no persons are required to respond to a collection of information unless it displays a valid OMB control number.
PTO Form 1478 (Rev 09/2006)
OMB No. 0651-0009 (Exp. 12/31/2014)

Trademark/Service Mark Application, Principal Register

Version 5.2

NOTE: This identifies who owns the mark, not necessarily who is filing the application. For an instructional video focusing on what is meant by the term "applicant," click here.

Applicant Information	
Note: This identifies who **owns** the mark, **not** necessarily who is **filing** the application. **Note**: If there is more than one owner of the mark, complete the information for the first owner, and then click on the "Add Owner" button at the bottom of this page. Repeat, as necessary, for the appropriate listing of all owners. Warning: It is important to determine whether, in fact, the applicants are joint applicants, or some other entity type listed below.	
* **Owner of Mark**	[If an individual, use the following format: Last Name, First Name Middle Initial or Name, if applicable]
☐ **DBA (doing business as)** ☐ **AKA (also known as)** ☐ **TA (trading as)** ☐ **Formerly**	
Entity Type ○ **Individual** ○ **Corporation** ○ **Limited Liability Company** ○ **Partnership** ○ **Limited Partnership** ○ **Joint Venture** ○ **Sole Proprietorship** ○ **Trust** ○ **Estate** ○ **Other**	**<== Click the appropriate circle on the left to indicate the applicant's entity type. The form will then display the field(s) for entering information corresponding to that specific entity type. If your entity type is not one of the options displayed directly to the left, you must click on "Other" and then select the appropriate entry from the relevant pull-down box.**
Internal Address	
* **Street Address**	**NOTE:** You must limit your entry here, and for all remaining fields within this overall section (except City, see *below*), to no more than 40 characters (the storage limit for the USPTO database). You may need to abbreviate some words, *e.g.*, St. instead of Street. Failure to do so may result in an undeliverable address, due to truncation at the 40 character limit.
* **City**	**NOTE:** You must limit your entry here to no more than 22 characters.
* **State** **(Required for U.S. applicants)**	Select State **NOTE:** You must include as part of the "city" entry any information related to geographical regions (*e.g.*, provinces) not found in the dropdown lists for "States" or "Countries." Enter the city and then the geographical region, separated by a comma (*e.g.*, Toronto, Ontario). In most instances, you will then also have to select the country within which the region is found, below.
* **Country or U.S. Territory**	Select Country or U.S. Territory

Business Plan Template

College Athlete, LLC

Overview

College Athlete, LLC's Business Plan outlines strategic initiatives to elevate brand visibility, expand market reach, and increase income.

This plan focuses on leveraging innovative marketing strategies to enhance College Athlete, LLC's position in the market.

Key Findings and Recommendations

- Identified opportunities for market expansion through targeted advertising and promotions.
- Recommendation to enhance digital marketing efforts to reach a wider audience.

Goals and Objectives

Brand Awareness

Increase brand awareness by 25% within the next year through a comprehensive marketing campaign.

Market Expansion

Increase market share by 15% through targeted promotions.

Revenue Growth

Achieve a 20% growth in revenue over the next two years.

Target Audience and Segmentation

Segment	Characteristics	Marketing Strategy
Segment 1 (Team Fans & Young Athletes)	Supporters of your team, ages 16-24, active on social media.	Social media campaigns, influencer partnerships.Share authentic, behind-the-scenes content and personal stories.
Segment 2 (Local Businesses)	Regional Businesses who support and are fans of the team. Community-oriented businesses.	Partner with local businesses for in-person appearances, and promote in local media outlets.
Segment 3 (National Brands & Businesses)	Larger companies, brands seeking athlete ambassadors, broader demographic.	Use professional media kits, connect via NIL platforms, and attend industry networking events.

Advertising and Promotions

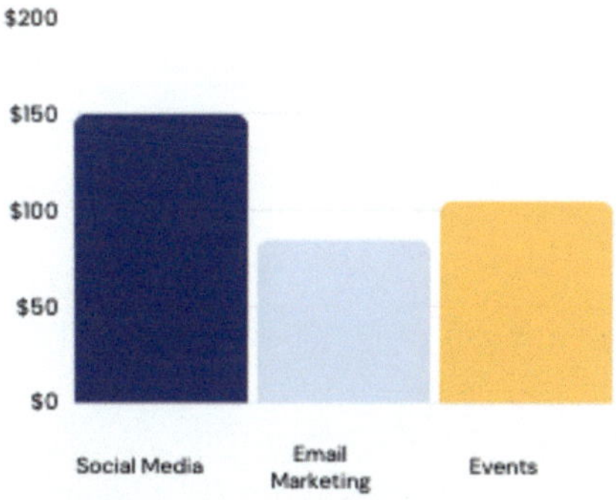

College Athlete, LLC

NIL Deal Tracker Sheet

Cedric Hopkins
123 Any Street
Columbus, Ohio 43209
530-564-2321

NIL DEAL TRACKER

COLLEGE ATHLETE, LLC

DEAL NAME/BRAND	DATE SIGNED	CONTRACT TERM	DELIVERABLES	PAYMENT	DUE DATE
NIKE					
BMW					
YETI					
SNICKERS					
APPLE					
THE HLO					

Targeted Sponsorship Outreach Email Template

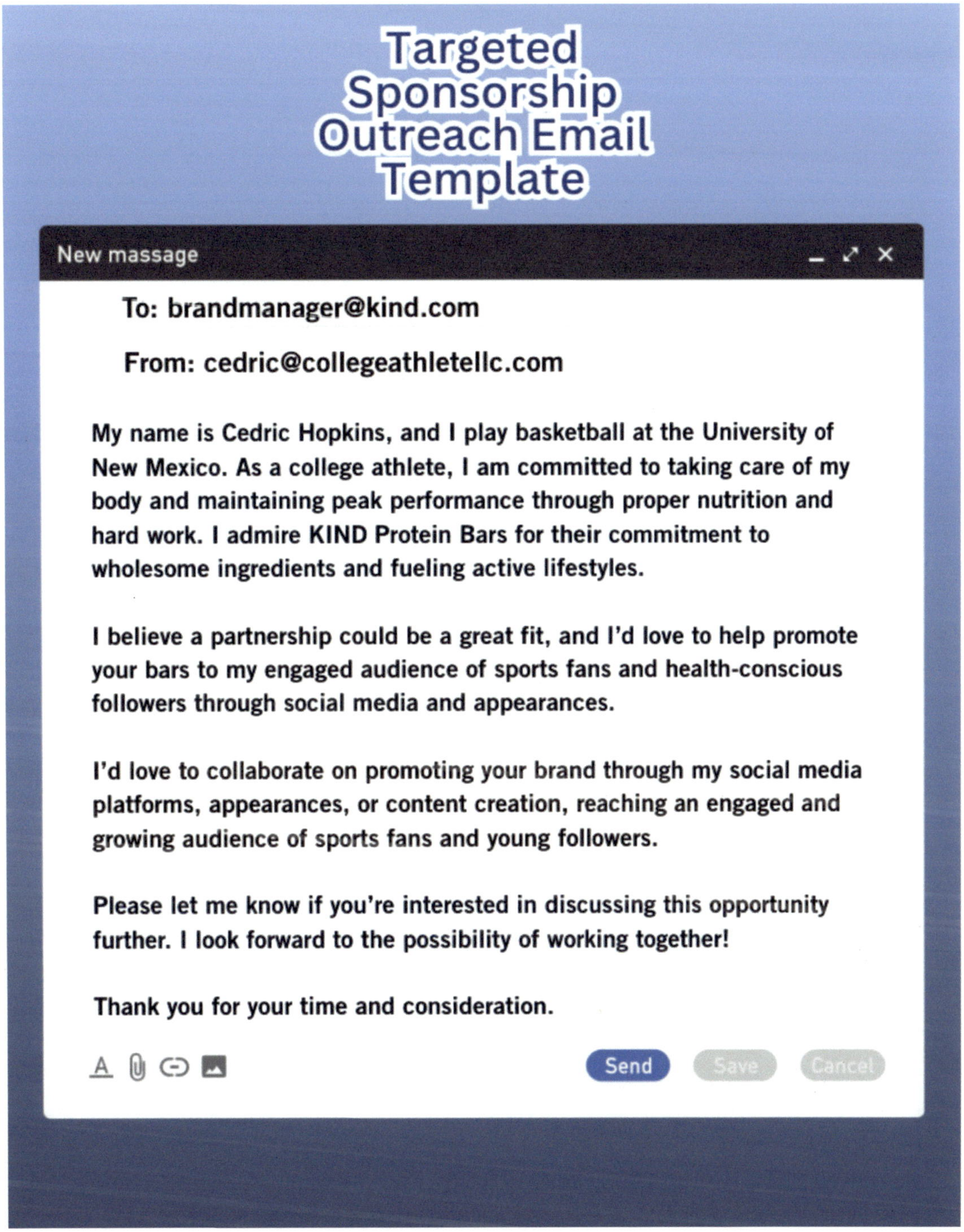

Targeted Sponsorship Outreach Email Template

New massage

To: brandmanager@kind.com

From: cedric@collegeathletellc.com

My name is Cedric Hopkins, and I play basketball at the University of New Mexico. As a college athlete, I am committed to taking care of my body and maintaining peak performance through proper nutrition and hard work. I admire KIND Protein Bars for their commitment to wholesome ingredients and fueling active lifestyles.

I believe a partnership could be a great fit, and I'd love to help promote your bars to my engaged audience of sports fans and health-conscious followers through social media and appearances.

I'd love to collaborate on promoting your brand through my social media platforms, appearances, or content creation, reaching an engaged and growing audience of sports fans and young followers.

Please let me know if you're interested in discussing this opportunity further. I look forward to the possibility of working together!

Thank you for your time and consideration.

Send Save Cancel

MY NOTES

MY NOTES

MY NOTES

MY NOTES

Made in the USA
Las Vegas, NV
03 November 2026

57424483R00119